Blood on Their Hands
The Hillary – Obama Standard

Danny Cox

ISBN:1534609873
ISBN-13:9781534609877

DEDICATION

This book is dedicated to all those who have been brutally slaughtered due to the feckless policies of the Obama – Clinton Administration. To the parents who had to watch as their children were slaughtered, tortured, raped and enslaved. To the millions who still live in fear.

CONTENTS

Forward

This is not a book I ever wanted to write. It is a book I felt I had to write. I am an American. I love my country. It hurts my heart to see what is happening to her. I am 57 years old. As an elementary student I had to practice what to do in the event of a nuclear attack. As a young child I watched the Civil Rights movement unfold on my parents black and white television set.

As a teenage boy growing up I watched the Vietnam protests. Burning flags, draft cards, and bras. I watched on television as soldiers, sailors, and airmen returned home to hate filled shouts and jeers. Through all of those events I was concerned, but still there was always a sense of optimism, people still felt their children would live better lives and have more opportunities than they had, the American Way.

I don't feel that sense of optimism now. I know many people feel that sense of concern. How have we come to this place? We have been headed in this direction for quite some time, but the past 8 years have tremendously accelerated the pace.

For 15 years now, I have been pretty much confined to a wheelchair. For the past couple of years pretty much confined to the house. It gives me a lot of time to study. A lot of time to pay attention to current events. I am not able to get out and protest. I am not able to run for office.

So it seems the only thing I can do is try to make my voice heard through this book.

Americans have always been skeptical of their politicians. History and our Founders have always shown that is a good thing. That is precisely what the First and Second Amendment were designed for.

We have reached a very dangerous time in the history of our country. The vast majority of the mainstream media have simply become the cheerleaders of politicians who share their ideology and critics of those who don't. Many simply parrot what they are told by politicians they like instead of doing their job and doing actual investigative journalism. In this book you will see not just a prime example of this, but also where some in the current administration have actually bragged of it. You will see an example of that in the chapter on Iran.

At the same time, we have reached another very dangerous point in our history. We have reached a place where the ends seem to justify the means. It seems too many people don't care if they are lied too as long as it is politicians who are on their side doing the lying. Since Time Magazine called Obama's "If you like your Dr. you can keep your Dr. If you like your Insurance you can keep your Insurance," the "Lie of the Year," I have seen so many Democratic Pundits and supporters say so what. At least he got healthcare passed? Really? Have we really fallen to that point?

This is my 5th book, however, if you haven't read my others you will soon discover I am not a professional author. Just someone who cares about God, Family, and Country. I probably don't write the way people are taught to write. I write the forward of each new book first. I make changes as the book takes shape. For the first time ever, after the book was completed, I went back and changed the forward due to current events. A couple of things had to be added to make the book complete. I decided the best place to do that in an effort to get the book back to publishing in time was to simply add these things to the forward.

In this book, I have tried to stay away from mention of Bill Clinton. This book is supposed to be about the past 8 years. This new report from The Daily Caller however must be mentioned. This is a big deal and probably will never be reported on by the mainstream media.

From The Daily Caller:

"Former President Bill Clinton collected $5.6 million in fees from GEMS Education, a Dubai-based company that teaches Sharia Law through its network of more than 100 schools in the Middle East, Asia and Africa, according to a Daily Caller News Foundation investigation.

The company's finances strictly adhere to "Sharia Finance," which includes giving "zakat," a religious tax of which one-eighth of the proceeds is dedicated to funding Islamic jihad.

The company also contributed millions of dollars to the Clinton Foundation. His biggest paycheck from the closely-held company — which is incorporated in the

Cayman Islands — was in 2014 when he pocketed $2.1 million."

Please, don't take my word for this. Go to the website and read it for yourself!

Read more: http://dailycaller.com/2016/08/03/exclusive-bill-clinton-got-millions-from-worlds-biggest-sharia-law-education-firm/#ixzz4GSd52HBg

Now you may ask why this is so important. Sharia Law is totally incompatible with our United States Constitution and with the values our Country stands for. Again don't take my word for it. I included the Constitution in this book. This is a picture of my Sharia Law Manual. Get one and read it.

When combined with the Clinton's ties to the Muslim Brotherhood and her support of the same, this is very concerning. Hillary's ties to the Brotherhood don't end there, you will see much more in the chapter on Egypt.

The next thing I feel I had to add is the story the Wall Street Journal just broke on the ransom payment to Iran. Yes, in spite of Obama's lies to the contrary it was a ransom payment. Why does it matter? Just another very real example of the attitude from Obama and Hillary of it doesn't matter what lie they tell, what laws they break provided they get their way. Yes this did break Federal Law. Yes it did violate the Constitution by going around Congress. Yes when caught, as usual Obama lied about it.

Chapter 1 - Russia

August 1, 2008, Ossetian separatists began shelling Georgian villages, with a sporadic response from Georgian peacekeepers in the region. To put an end to these deadly attacks and restore order, the Georgian Army was sent to the South Ossetian conflict zone on August 7, 2008. Georgians took control of most of Tskhinvali, a separatist stronghold, in hours.

Russia accused Georgia of "aggression against South Ossetia", and officially launched a large-scale land, air and sea operation against Georgia on August 8, 2008 supposedly to bring peace to the area. Russian and Ossetian forces battled Georgian forces throughout South Ossetia for four days, with the heaviest fighting in Tskhinvali, until Georgian forces retreated. Russian and Abkhaz forces then attacked the Kodori Gorge, held by Georgia. Russian naval forces also blockaded part of the Georgian coast.

President of France Nicolas Sarkozy negotiated a ceasefire agreement on August 12, 2008. Russian forces temporarily occupied the Georgian cities of Zugdidi, Senaki, Poti, and Gori. Gori was actually invaded and occupied after the ceasefire was in place. The Russian military raided all the Georgian military bases in the area. The South Ossetians destroyed most ethnic Georgian villages in South Ossetia. Then they began a program of ethnic cleansing of Georgians. Russia recognized Abkhazia and South Ossetia as separate republics on August 26, 2008. Then the Georgian government immediately stopped diplomatic relations with Russia. Russia withdrew most of its troops from Georgia, except the disputed area October 8, 2008. This happened at the end of the George W. Bush Presidency.

Vladimir Putin is an intelligent man. He knew President Bush was a lame duck President. He knew the U.S. citizens were war weary. He knew without a strong U.S. President to lead, very little would be done to Russia by the International Community. He was right.

The short war created 192,000 refugees. As of 2014 there were still 20,272 refugees. The Russian military has increased its presence in Abkhazia and South Ossetia in violation of the ceasefire agreement of August 2008.

Even though Dmitry Anat.olyevich Medvedev was elected President of Russia on March 2, 2008, the invasion of Georgia was planned before Medvedev took office. It was always believed Medvedev was merely a puppet of Putin.

Tuesday, January 20, 2009, Barack H. Obama was sworn in as President of The United States of America. Putin and Medvedev had guessed right. The war weary American voters had elected a weak President.

On Feb. 2, 2009 Vice President Biden swore in Secretary of State Hillary Rodham Clinton. On March 6, 2009, the new Secretary of State met with her Russian counterpart, Russian Foreign Minister Sergey Lavrov in Geneva. Before sitting down to their working dinner, she presented him a small green box with a ribbon. Lavrov opened it and, inside, there was a red button with the Russian word "peregruzka" printed on it.

"I would like to present you with a little gift that represents what President Obama and Vice President Biden and I have been saying and that is: 'We want to reset our relationship, and so we will do it together.' "We worked hard to get the right Russian word. Do you think we got it?" she asked Lavrov, laughing.

"You got it wrong," said Lavrov, as both diplomats laughed. "It should be "perezagruzka" said Lavrov."This says 'peregruzka,' which means 'overcharged.

Merely months after Russia invaded Georgia, killed many Georgian civilians, displaced many more, Hillary Clinton was in Geneva laughing it up with her Russian Counterpart. Again Putin and Medvedev were right. Not only did Obama and Clinton do nothing to help Georgia, they actually rewarded Putin and Medvedev. It would be far from the last time.

In 2009, President Obama cancelled the deal the U.S. had with Poland and the Czech Republic to build an interceptor site and radar that would provide protection of the U.S. homeland and allies from rogue ballistic missiles. This was a deal made by President Bush and NATO to protect against missile launches from primarily Iran. It angered Russia and Putin.

On Friday, March 15, 2013 Obama and Clinton once again showed weakness and caved in to Putin. This time it was the 4th phase of the deal. A missile shield to protect our allies as well as our country. Canceling this angered Poland. They knew when they aligned themselves with the U.S.A. and NATO, it would anger Putin. This was the reason they had negotiated for the shield. Obama and Clinton caved. It sold out our allies, made us less safe and insured Putin and Russia would continue aggressions. If you remember Obama was caught with a "hot mike" telling Medvedev to tell Vladimir to be patient. That he, (Obama) would have more flexibility after his re-election. Look at the way he misused his 'flexibility."

It gets worse, much worse. How does one make $145,000,000.00 in a short time? Apparently it is very easy if you are Secretary of State. Your husband is a former President, and you have no ethics, no morals, and you don't mind selling the security of your country.

Bill and Hillary Clinton had helped a Canadian financier named Frank Giustra and a small Canadian company obtain a lucrative uranium mining concession from the dictator in Kazakhstan. The same Canadian company, renamed Uranium One, bought uranium concessions in the United States;

The Russian government wanted to buy that Canadian company for a price that would mean big profits for the Canadian investors. In order for the Russians to buy that Canadian company, it would require the approval of the Obama administration, including Hillary's State Department, because uranium is a strategically important commodity.

The deal was approved, the U.S.A. lost 20% of its uranium reserves, the top 9 investors in Uranium One donated $145,000,000.00 to the Clintons. Don't take my word for it. Do your own research. Even the extremely liberal New York Times did a 3,000 word expose' on the deal. Of course in the more than one year since the front page New York Times article, we have heard nothing from the mainstream media about this.

This is by no means the only deal that should be investigated. Had you or I attempted something like this we would reside in a Federal Pennitentary.

This policy of appeasement of Russia and Putin also complicated our policy in regard to Syria, Iran, and Yemen, as you will see in other chapters. The deals made by the Clintons with other countries will also be detailed as we go through the book.

Chapter 2 - Iran

One could almost write this book just on Iran. From not supporting the Iranian dissidents in 2009 to the horrible nuclear deal, to our naval personal being captured and humiliated. Iran violating the deal almost before the ink was dried. Iran supporting and financing Hezbollah, the Houthi rebels in Yemen, the Shia militias in Iraq and the list goes on.

I think one of the most dangerous lies told by this administration had to do with the Iranian nuclear deal. Yes I know the deal was actually signed after Hillary resigned from the State Department but Hillary's fingerprints are all over it.

In an eye-opening article in the New York Times by David Samuels, senior White House officials bragged about how they used both lazy and friendly reporters to push their propaganda about the "deal." Not only reporters they also bragged of using nonprofits to push President Obama's horrible and dangerous foreign policy. They also claimed they can do it almost at will because these people are ignorant, and will believe what they're told. Rhodes even claimed they will pretty much take whatever he tells them as truth and push the agenda.

In the article Samuels said they admitted they were misleading the American people about the deal. That the negotiations actually started a year before it was announced. It also appears the claims Iran had a new "more moderate" leadership was not only false, but they knew it was.

Ben Rhodes even had the audacity to admit this quote from the article, "The average reporter we talk to is 27 years old, and their only reporting experience consists of being around political campaigns," Rhodes says. "They literally know nothing."

Then there is the following quote from a Rhodes assistant Ned Price. He was talking about what he called "force multipliers," more senior reporters and pundits who parrot what they're told. "I'll give them some color," Price says, using the journalistic term for juicy bits of inside information, "and the next thing I know, lots of these guys are in the dot-com publishing space, and have huge Twitter followings, and they'll be putting this message out on their own."

White House digital information head Tanya Somanader, was quoted as saying. "Laura Rozen was my RSS feed," Somanader tells Samuels. "She would just find everything and retweet it."

Because the Iran deal was so unpopular with the American people, Congress and the Senate, they knew they would have their work cut out for them. Rhodes, Obama, and Hillary wanted this deal done regardless. It mattered not one bit the will of the People, the three of them wanted their way. So they established a "war room" before the American people had any idea their government was in negotiations with the world's leading state sponsor of terrorism, Iran.

Ben Rhodes, the man whose desire was to become a fiction writer achieved his desires. He was certainly writing fiction about the Iran deal. They decided the only hope getting the deal was to frame it as if we don't do the deal the only other option is war. So that was the narrative pushed from the war room. Any criticism for the deal was met with "the only other option is war" lie.

The sanctions were working. The Iranian people were getting restless and wanted a change in leadership. The Iranian economy was in the toilet. Had the three stooges given verbal encouragement to the Iranian dissidents in 2009, and stayed the course with the sanctions, we quite possibly may have seen a change in the Iranian leadership. That would not have fit the narrative these 3 and later John Kerry desired. They wanted the narrative Obama stopped the Iranian nukes without a war.

The more the details come out about the deal, the more we see how we were lied to. It is important here to remember they were helped in this endeavor by the media and liberal "think tanks."

More quotes from the interview:

"We created an echo chamber," Rhodes tells Samuels about the journalists and think-tankers who were discussing the Iran deal based on information given to them by the White House. "They were saying things that validated what we had given them to say. "I mean, I'd prefer a sober, reasoned public debate, after which members of Congress reflect and take a vote," he told Samuels. "But that's impossible." Ben Rhodes writing more fiction!

In the end, 58 senators voted against the deal. That means once again to get their way, they went around the will of the people. Around the will of the Senate. Around the will of Congress.

One other point to consider. Given what we now know from Rhodes and his assistants bragging, at the time U.S. troops were still in Iraq having to fight against Iranian funded militias, Rhodes, Hillary, Obama, and company were negotiating with the enemy. How does that make you feel?

Hillary's fingerprints are all over at least the beginning of this deal. After leaving her position she still championed the deal in speeches and interviews. The question the American voter must ask. Did she do it because she believe in it? Did she lie to the American people about it just for Obama's support in the 2016 election? In other words, did she lie to the American people because she thinks she, Obama, Rhodes, and Kerry know better than the American people? Or even worse, did she lie to the

American people even though she knew it was a horrible deal but wanted Obama's support in 2016? Does she want to be President so much that she would endanger the safety of America? The safety of Israel? The safety of the world? If so, is that the kind of person you want as your President?

Hillary calls herself a champion of women's rights. A champion of the LGBT community. A champion of the oppressed. Really? How then can she champion this horrible bill with a country who hangs members of the LGBT community from cranes? Two men, Abdullah Ghavami Chahzanjiru and Salman Ghanbari Chahzanjiri, were hanged from cranes in southern Iran on August 6, 2014, for consensual sodomy.

Their deaths are part of a wave of executions in Iran, with more than 400 in the first half of 2014 alone, according to the NGO Iran Human Rights. 400 in 6 months!

Women's rights are severely restricted in Iran. Legally, the following laws apply to women in the Islamic Republic of Iran:

The husband is the head of the family, and his wife is legally bound to obey him. Article 1105 of the civil code states: "In relations between husband and wife, the position of the head of the family exclusively belongs to the husband."

A married woman cannot leave the country without her husband's permission.

A woman's testimony as a witness is worth half that of a man, in compliance with the sharia basis of the legal system.

In all public places, women must wear a hijab and loose fitting clothing.

Polygamy and temporary marriage are permitted for men up to four wives are allowed, but not for women.

Women are frequently subject to honor killings. In cases where the father kills his daughter, he is not liable for the death penalty, but only for imprisonment. When someone is murdered, the family of the victim can forgive the murderer. Usually that means when a family member honor kills a woman, the family forgives them. Under normal circumstances if the family forgives the law forgives.

As in Saudi Arabia, Iran has morality police. These so called morality police are made from volunteer members of the Basij militia who patrol the streets enforcing Islamic Sharia law in public spaces. The Basij also routinely detain young, unmarried women found talking or being friendly with any men except relatives. Basically they are men who volunteer to enforce Sharia Law. Yet Hillary, Obama, and Kerry are champions of women's rights? They lie to the American people in order to get a bad deal with a regime who treats women like this?

Could part of the reasons stem from this? The Clinton Foundation received a large donation from the Alavi Foundation, a front for the Iranian regime that sought to advance the regime's point of view. Alavi's financial disclosures show a $30,000 donation in 2005. Could part of it come from Obama's top advisor, Iranian born Valerie Jarrett? Jarrett is is an American government official who is Senior Advisor to the President of the United States and Assistant to the President for Public Engagement and Intergovernmental Affairs in the Obama administration. She is a Chicago lawyer, businesswoman, and civic leader. Before that she served as a co-chair of the Obama–Biden Transition Project.

If you have never read them, I encourage you to read any of Randy L. Noble's books. They can be found on Amazon. He also has a blog talk radio channel, "The Cross in The Desert" and you can follow him on twitter @randyforiran. Randy is a Christian author and human rights activist for Iran. See what it is like for women who are forced to live under Sharia Law in Iran.

Chapter 3 - Afghanistan

I saved this chapter as the last one to write. I did this because this may be the country the Obama – Hillary agenda has been morally the worst.

In late summer of 2002, I had the pleasure of meeting a retired Russian Major. I was able to spend some time drinking coffee and talking about the war in Afghanistan and the World Trade Tower attack. The Major had spent over two years fighting with the Russian Army in Afghanistan. Many of the things he told me about the Taliban chilled me to the bone.

He told of Russian soldiers who after they were captured were brutally tortured. After the Taliban felt they had all the information they were going to get they would stake the soldier to the ground. Then cut their stomach open, pull their intestines out and place them on the soldier's chest. Then watch as the soldier died a very slow, very painful death.

He told of the child brides and the hell on earth they endure. How little girls were raped, killed, or have acid thrown in their faces. He was the first person I heard the term "The Dancing Boys of Afghanistan" from. Since then I have heard way too much about them. The Taliban believe young boys are for "pleasure" young girls to have babies. As long as the young boy hasn't reached puberty they believe it is permissible to use them as sex slaves.

The Major proved to be very prophetic. He said America had the most powerful, best military the world had ever seen. He also said we would probably never defeat the Taliban. Not because we couldn't. He said our military could defeat the Taliban in less than a year. He said we probably wouldn't though because of our liberal media and weak politicians. He said the media would never tell the truth of how evil and brutal the Taliban really is. The weak politicians would not truly unleash the military to defeat the Taliban. The American public would get war weary and elect anti-war politicians. Sound familiar?

Those of you old enough to remember the cold war may be asking how I could believe what a Russian military officer said. Remember the video that was smuggled out of Afghanistan in 2001 of the woman in a Burka on the ground in a packed soccer stadium. Remember watching as a Taliban savage approached her from behind with an AK-47 and shot her in the back of the head? Remember hearing the crowd celebrate the killing of this woman with cheers and shouts of Allah Akbar? I do. That is how I could believe him.

Some of you may also be asking what this has to do with the past 8 years of Obama and Hillary. Stay with me, I'm getting there.

The next true story about Afghanistan. I have a friend I met in 1983 who has been fighting in Afghanistan since 2002, both as a soldier and as a contractor. I have trusted my life to this man in the past, and would again.

About 3 years ago was the last time we spoke. I pray every day he is safe. I pray every day God will heal his heart.

I will never forget him telling me how this war had changed him. He said he reads my Facebook posts and appreciates my efforts to educate people. He also told me from what I post I know more than most about the evil that is the Taliban, but that even I have no idea how bad.

He said seeing the brutality one human could be to another had forever changed him. He stays year after year and does what he does to fight that evil. To defend our country and try to do his part to keep that evil from coming to America.

He stays year after year to do his part to defend the innocent civilians of Afghanistan who have no choice but living in Afghanistan. He said no one can imagine the hell on earth they are forced to live with. The stoning, be-heading, rapes, torture, sex slaves and other horrors. Parents being forced to watch as their children are executed by the savages known as the Taliban.

Schools attacked and the children slaughtered. Women being forced to watch as their husbands are slaughtered then given to a Taliban "Holy Warrior" to be used as a sex slave. The rape of little boys. It is heartbreaking. His words will forever impact my heart.

In an April 2013 report by Reuters, as many as 74 school girls at the Bibi Hawa Girls High School were poisoned after falling sick from smelling a strange gas. The school, located in Taluquan, the capital of Afghanistan's far North province of Takhar, was only the latest incident of mass poisonings of girls schools a tragedy being coordinated by the ultra-conservative elements of the Afghan Taliban believe girls should not be educated.

As of April 2013 the Afghan Education Ministry has closed 550 schools across the country due to security concerns, affecting 300,000 students in eleven provinces.

That poisoning came three days after another girls school in Taluquan was reportedly gassed, sending a dozen young girls to the hospital.

Taluquan's schools witnessed four similar poisonings on girls' schools between May and June of 2012, poisoning 700 girls through contaminated drinking water and poisonous gas, prompting provincial officials mandating principals of schools to instruct staff and faculty to remain on the grounds after students' dismissal, and inspect the schools for any suspicious objects or activity. One such poisoning on May 23, 2012 affected 120 girls on the same day, and another poisoning of a local boys' school sickened 200 students.

The most recent data I could find shows over 700 attacks per year on Afghan girl schools and or students.

One lady who runs a girls school said they have to send adults into the restrooms on breaks to make sure none of the students drink water from the plumbing. They had to dig a well because it is the only way to trust the water hasn't been poisoned. The well is guarded and still a man must drink from it every morning to insure it wasn't poisoned overnight.

The janitor and teachers have to come in early every day to test the air. Human guinea pigs. They have to walk through the schools opening windows even during the cold of winter to let the school air out before the students arrive. They must have armed guards. Can you imagine having to endure that just to get an education?

Even with all the precautions and security, schools are still poisoned. They are still bombed and attacked by the Taliban. Students are kidnapped and married off to the Taliban. They are shot. They have acid thrown in their faces. They are slaughtered. Their families are slaughtered.

Now we get to what all the above has to do with the Obama – Hillary Administration.

Let us remember this is the Administration that accuses the Republican Party of a war on women. An Administration that considers itself as champions of women's rights and education. Hillary considers herself a champion of women's rights and asks for your vote because she has shattered the glass ceiling.

Why then would she negotiate with the Taliban? If she really cared about women's rights would she negotiate with savages who allow women no rights? If she truly cared about education would she negotiate with savages who kill, rape and maim to prevent children, especially female children, from getting an education?

Let's face reality. The only possible reason is to help keep the Democratic promise of ending the wars. What kind of person can negotiate with these savages and look at themselves in the mirror? What kind of person can look the American people in the eye and proclaim to be a women's rights hero, while negotiating with these savages?

It is not just Hillary. It starts at the top. First with Obama, then Hillary, now Kerry. You can't make a deal with the Devil. There is no negotiating with evil. Either you destroy the evil or it destroys you.

Chapter 4 - Egypt

The Egyptian revolution of 2011, began on January 25, 2011 and took place across all of Egypt. There were demonstrations, marches, occupations of plazas, riots, non-violent civil resistance, acts of civil disobedience and strikes. Millions of protesters from a range of socio-economic and religious backgrounds demanded the overthrow of Egyptian President Hosni Mubarak. The revolution included Islamic, liberal, anti-capitalist, nationalist and feminist elements. Violent clashes between security forces and protesters resulted in at least 846 people killed and over 6,000 injured. Protesters burned over 90 police stations. The protests took place in Cairo, Alexandria and other cities.

It was part of the so called Arab Spring. Mubarak had long been a US Ally and had kept a peace treaty with

Israel. This is not to say he was a good guy, he wasn't but he did keep the terrorist under control. He did keep peace with Israel.

Under pressure domestically and internationally, including the Obama – Hillary Administrations, Mubarak stepped down on Feb. 11, 2011.

The Army established a Supreme Council to rule Egypt until a new Constitution could be written and elections conducted.

June 24, 2012, Muslim Brotherhood candidate Mohamed Morsi, the first Islamist elected head of an Arab state, was declared the winner of the presidential election by the Egyptian electoral commission.

In spite of his campaign promises to the contrary, Morsi almost immediately begin trying to implement parts of Sharia Law. Trying to purge the Military of secular leaders. In general trying to make Egypt more like an Islamic Theocracy. The people of Egypt again begin to protest. After a while the Military stepped again and deposed Morsi. Morsi and many other Muslim Brotherhood leaders were arrested.

President Obama and his Administration, Hillary and the State Department had all supported Morsi after his election. So much in fact a number of private citizens in Egypt filed a flurry of lawsuits with the International Criminal Court (ICC) that named world leaders, including President Obama and Hillary Clinton, in 2013.

But those lawsuits were dismissed in 2014 because the citizens who filed them were not authorized to do so.

A professor of criminal law named Nabil Medhat Salem filed one of those lawsuits. The lawsuit, filed in August of 2013, named President Obama and members of the Muslim Brotherhood, the Cairo Post reported:

"Medhat has accused the Brotherhood leaders of deliberately killing numerous citizens at Rabaa al – Adawiya and Nahda Squares, burning mosques and churches, and he accused Obama of participating in these violent acts through incitement and support."

The ICC dismissed the claims in 2014 because Medhat and other private citizens were not authorized to file the lawsuits.

It is important to note the Egyptian people were so upset with Obama and Hillary for their support of Morsi and the Muslim Brotherhood, not only did they try to sue them in the ICC they tried their best to have the Egyptian Government prosecute them criminally for supporting a terrorist organization.

On Sunday, July 15, 2012, on a trip to Egypt to reopen a US Consulate in Alexandria and to meet with and congratulate President Morsi, Egyptian protesters threw tomatoes and shoes at U.S. Secretary of State Hillary Clinton's motorcade and shouted, "Monica, Monica, Monica" as she left the newly reopened U.S. Consulate in Alexandria.

Clinton said she was in the city to answer critics who believe Washington has taken sides in Egyptian politics. There were already vocal protesters at the start of her visit to the consulate, forcing the ceremony to be moved inside.

Even at that early time the Egyptians believe she and President Obama had much to do with the election of Morsi and the Muslim Brotherhood.

Christians and other minorities had not had it easy under Mubarak, but much better than under Morsi. Almost immediately after Morsi's election attacks on Christians and other religious minorities increased tremendously. Christian girls began being kidnapped and forced to convert to Islam and marry a Muslim man. Churches and Christian businesses were attacked. Of course this happens anywhere, anytime the Muslim Brotherhood is in control.

Finally the Egyptian Army had enough. The Egyptian people had enough and the Military took control from Morsi. Obama and Hillary were not happy with the actions of the Egyptian Military.

President Obama's official statement about the overthrow of Morsi was, "The United States continues to believe firmly that the best foundation for lasting stability in Egypt is a democratic political order with participation from all sides and all political parties — secular and religious, civilian and military. During this uncertain period, we expect the military to ensure that the rights of all Egyptian men and women are protected, including the right to peaceful assembly, due process, and free and fair trials in civilian courts. Moreover, the goal of any political process should be a government that respects the rights of all people, majority and minority; that institutionalizes the checks and balances upon which democracy depends; and that places the interests of the people above party or faction. The voices of all those who have protested peacefully must be heard – including those who welcomed today's developments, and those who have supported President Morsi. In the interim, I urge all sides to avoid violence and come together to ensure the lasting restoration of Egypt's democracy."

It was during this time another link to Hillary was discovered. A senior Muslim Brotherhood operative, Gehad (Jihad) el-Haddad was arrested in Egypt. Gehad (Jihad) el-Haddad. worked for years at the William J. Clinton Foundation. The Clinton Foundation has also received millions of dollars from Saudi Arabia, Qatar and a foundation that is an Iranian regime front.

From 2007 to 2012, el-Haddad was the Egyptian director for the Clinton Foundation. El-Haddad's father is Essam el-Haddad, a member of the Brotherhood's Guidance Bureau.

While he worked for the Clintons, El-Haddad began working in May 2011 as a senior adviser for the Egyptian Muslim Brotherhood's political wing, the Freedom and Justice Party. Evidently, the Clinton Foundation had no problem with his side-work because they continued to employ him. One month after El-Haddad left the Foundation, Morsi spoke at the Clinton Global Initiative.

Where does this support for the Muslim Brotherhood come from? An organization whose stated goal is to take over the United States and dominate the world. None of us can say for sure. It is a safe bet to say however at least some of it comes from Huma Abedin.

The Clarion Project has reported extensively on Abedin, such as how she served as an assistant-editor of an Islamist journal from 1996, when she became a White House intern, until 2008, when she became Deputy Chief of Staff to Hillary Clinton, then-Secretary of State. The journal was put together by several members of Abedin's immediate family, including her mother, a prominent member of the Muslim Sisterhood.

Chapter 5 – Libya

One of Hillary's biggest failures as Secretary of State has to be Libya. It was supposed to be her crowning achievement and catapult her into the Whitehouse in 2016. How ironic it has become one of the most defining events to show why she should never again be allowed to reside at 1600 Pennsylvania Avenue.

In the interest of full disclosure I have read the book 13 hours. I have also seen the movie. Since I have I am only going to touch very briefly on Benghazi. I do encourage every American to read the book and watch the movie. How anyone can watch the movie, read the book, and read the 800 page House report on Benghazi, and still vote for anyone who had anything to do with allowing Benghazi to happen, then lie about it escapes me.

The one thing I will say about Benghazi is I strongly believe the most damaging events regarding Benghazi have still not been made public. In my heart I truly believe before all is said and done on Benghazi, the American people will see Obama and Hillary were using

Benghazi and Libya to supply weapons to ISIS and other Islamic Terrorists.

There is so much information available on the events regarding Libya, anyone with the desire could write a large book just on that. After a year of research, reading pro- Hillary reporting, anti-Hillary reporting, pro-Obama reporting, anti-Obama reporting, released emails and leaked emails, I am certain of one thing. No Hillary, no US Military intervention in Libya.

Everything points to Hillary. Obama was very skeptical of getting involved. He had after all been elected on getting the US out of wars in that region. The vast majority of his advisors were against getting involved. Hillary eventually swayed the President to get involved. She believed there would be a humanitarian crisis in and around Benghazi if we didn't intervene. She felt that would be a huge PR nightmare. Not something one desires when they have their eye on a Presidential run.

She wanted to arm the Libyan Rebels who were fighting Qaddafi. The opposition leaders wanted something more immediate. They wanted weapons.

The rebels seemed unable to get past Brega, an oil port on the way to Tripoli, and they said weapons from the Americans would help them to be able to defeat Qaddafi once and for all. The idea of arming the Rebels was causing a tremendous debate among Obama's advisors.

For one thing rumors were coming back of the horrible civil rights abuses of some of the Rebels when they would take over a new area. For another thing our own Intelligence Officials admitted they were unable to determine who the "good Rebels" were, and which ones were Islamists taking advantage of the turmoil.

Qatar and the United Arab Emirates had been supplying the rebels with weapons. Hillary argued Qatar was sending arms only to militias from the city of Misurata and select Islamist brigades. She argued this could further destabilize things after the fall of Qaddafi and give terrorist another base from which to work.

She also argued if the US did not arm the Rebels we would have little if any credibility in Libya after the fall.

NATO's supreme allied commander, Adm. James G. Stavridis, had told Congress of "flickers" of Al Qaeda within the opposition. She was still being told by Intelligence leaders they simply did not know enough about which Rebels would be safe enough to arm.

There was a reason to worry. A French shipment of missiles and machine guns had recently ended up going to a militia led by Abdel Hakim Belhaj, a militant Islamist. Still Hillary persisted and once again swayed President Obama to begin covertly arming the Rebels.

When Qaddafi finally fell, hacked emails now released show her trusted friend and advisor Sidney Blumenthal, who regularly emailed her political advice and intelligence reports on Libya, urged her to capitalize on the dictator's fall.

"You must go on camera. You must establish yourself in the historical record at this moment." He said in one email.

In a speech before the National Defense University she bragged of the use of "smart power" in Libya. She went on to say, ""For the first time we have a NATO-Arab alliance taking action, you've got Arab countries who are running strike actions," she said. "This is exactly the kind of world that I want to see where it's not just the United States and everybody is standing on the sidelines while we bear the cost, while we bear the sacrifice."

She was so proud of herself! Her crowning achievement! She just knew this would carry her all the way to the Whitehouse. Instead it may prove to be her Waterloo.

What began as a campaign that was only to save civilian lives in Benghazi and was only to have lasted 10 days, ended in yet another failed State. It ended in the deaths of a US Ambassador Chris Stevens, Sean Smith, Glenn Doherty, and Tyrone Woods. It ended up with an ISIS Army of 8,000 strong in Libya. A strong Al Qaeda presence, and in 2016 the U.S bombing in Libya once again.

Did it also end up arming ISIS in Syria? Time will tell.

Chapter 6 - Nigeria

In 2009 I began sending email's to Hillary's State Department asking, pleading, and documenting the need to have Boko Haram listed on the State Department Terror list. I could never understand why Boko Haram was left off the list so long. It allowed them to grow into a major terror organization. Nor could I understand why the Kerry State Department added Boko Haram as quickly as it did in light of Hillary's refusal. Could this have anything to do with her refusal?

In May of 2015, Judicial Watch issued a statement regarding this. Senator David Vitter is also investigating it. A developer from Nigeria, Gilbert Chagoury, donated about $5,000,000.00 to the Clintons during the time Hillary was refusing to add Boko Haram to the Terror List. Was this the reason for her refusal? A developer certainly doesn't need the publicity of a major terrorist group operating in the same area as his developments.

Perhaps it is innocent. No way can I prove it either way. Anyone can google his name, see his past, and come to their own conclusion. Where there is so much smoke, there is usually fire.

While Boko Haram was allowed to grow into a major terror operation, many Christians and others were paying a heavy price. A look at some of the worst atrocities while Hillary delayed.

In January of 2010, Boko Haram attacked 2 Christian Churches in Jos. Both Pastors were killed. At least 45 Christians were slaughtered and 100 wounded.

On March 7, 2010, we had our first real sign the Fulani Herdsman and Boko Haram were beginning to work together some. Those of us who follow these things had suspected it. This next attack prompted me to send another email to the Hillary State Department asking again to have Boko Haram listed as a Terror Organization and explaining why I felt the merger was imminent with the Fulani and Boko Haram.

In the early morning hours the Christian village of Dogo Nahauwa, Nigeria was attacked. Eyewitnesses reported the Fulani Muslim militants were chanting 'Allah Akbar,' broke into houses, cutting human beings, including children and women with their knives, machetes and swords, and burning others to death.. Other than the sheer number of victims what was so different this time? Many of the attackers were armed with fully automatic AK-47's. This was far from normal for the Fulani. In order for this to happen, either Boko Haram provided the weapons, and or provided some of their "Holy Warriors."

More than 500 mainly Christians were brutally murdered. More than 600 wounded. Still silence from the State Department. Still no movement on having Boko Haram added to the list. Why?

From March 8 – July 17, 2010, in a combined effort by Boko Haram and the Fulani Herdsman more than 109 mostly Christian, and mostly women and children were killed. Many of whom were burned to death or brutally hacked to death. One Pastor of a Church of Christ Church lost his wife and children. Many Churches were destroyed.

December 24 - 25, 2010, Boko Haram attacked a series of Christian villages in Nigeria. They killed 86 and wounded 74 primarily Christians. Bombs were set off in a busy market where people were finishing their Christmas shopping. A Baptist pastor and two choir members preparing for a late-night carol service were hacked to death inside one Church. Churches were bombed as Christians celebrated Christmas. Still Hillary and her State Department remained silent.

On April 17 and 18 of 2011, more than 300 primarily Christians were slaughtered and over 600 wounded. Many were hacked to death, some burnt to death and some taken down with automatic weapons fire, another sign of Boko Haram involvement. Many homes and Churches were burnt to the ground, some with people in them. Still there was no movement on the terror list from the Clinton/Obama State Department. I personally sent another email after this event. The death toll continued to climb. The State Department remained silent.

In October of 2012 at least twenty-six Christian students are singled out and executed by Islamists at their campus. Some are shot, others have their throats cut. In August of 2012, Boko Haram "Holy Warriors" enter a church and open up on members with machine-guns, killing at least nineteen, including the pastor. Two politicians are among twenty-three Christians, including women and children, killed by Boko Haram during a funeral for other victims of Islamic terror.

Still no news on adding Boko Haram, so just like when Cancer goes untreated it grows, Boko Haram grew. They became even more brutal, better armed and grew in number. The land area they controlled grew in size. They swore their allegiance to ISIS.

In April of 2014, Boko Haram had grown to the point they kidnapped an estimated 270 young school girls. You remember this. The US started a Twitter campaign, #BringBackOurGirls. Remember the picture of Mrs. Obama holding up the Bring Back Our Girls sign? Abubakar Shekau, the leader of Boko Haram released a 30 minute video of him standing in front of over 100 of the young girls. In that video he mocked The First Lady for her Twitter post. He also mocked the President and the U.S.A. He also made the Christian girls say the Shahada. The Shahada is the Muslim profession of Faith. It is all a non-Muslim has to do to become a Muslim.

Translated from Arabic the words in the Shahada are: "There is no god but God and Muhammad is his messenger."

This means if any of those young girls were to escape and make it back to their Christian families, they would still be Muslim. If they tried to go back to their Christian beliefs they would be considered Apostates from Islam. As such, according to Sharia that Boko Haram wants established, they should be killed immediately.

In the 12 months after that kidnapping, Amnesty International says Boko Haram kidnapped at least 2,000 additional women and girls.

So yes Hillary, your words about the Republican war on women mean absolutely nothing to me. You and you alone kept Boko Haram off the Terrorist list. They may have still grown to the same size and done the same things if they were on the list but we will never know the answer to that thanks to you. We, the American citizens are told by the State Department that list is an effective tool. If so why didn't you utilize it?

How do you sleep at night Hillary?

Chapter 7 - Iraq and Syria

I combined these two countries together because the same policies contributed to both. As you will see it also contributed to the wave of Islamic terrorism around the world. Including terror attacks in the USA including San Bernardino and Orlando.

We go back to 2011. Obama had made a campaign promise to get out of the war in Iraq. All the Generals were advising keeping 20,000 troops in Iraq to keep Iraq secure. They kept negotiating the amount down. Finally the Generals said they could do it with 10,000. Obama didn't want that either.

On December 18, 2011 the last convoy of American troops crossed into Kuwait. Obama tried to have it both ways. He said he ended the war. He brought the troops home. He covered his bases though by saying because he couldn't get the Iraqi's to sign a Status of Forces Agreement. The reality is he didn't try hard enough because he wanted out. He wasn't the only one, so did Hillary.

Hillary was a leading and outspoken supporter of the Obama administration's decision to withdraw U.S. forces from Iraq and even defended the White House's controversial failure to reach a status of forces agreement with the Iraqi government. She made the rounds to most of the news outlets defending Obama and talking about how great it was. Of course she even tried to blame George W. Bush for her and Obama's failure.

In a 2011 interview with CNN 2011 she said "we have a lot of presence in that region." She added that countries such as Iran should not "miscalculate about our continuing commitment to and with the Iraqis going forward."

She said in another interview, said the Obama administration has "a plan in place" to ensure Iraq's security. "Are the Iraqis all going to get along with each other for the foreseeable future? Well, let's find out."

Hillary, in a separate interview with NBC's David Gregory in 2011 said, "We are providing a support-and-training mission. We will be there on the ground working with the Iraqis. And I just want to add, David, that no one should miscalculate America's resolve and commitment to helping support the Iraqi democracy. We have paid too high a price to give the Iraqis this chance and I hope that Iran and no one else miscalculates that."

Clinton also praised Obama's "great leadership" in the interview. "We know that the violence is not going to automatically end, but President Obama has shown great leadership in navigating to this point, fulfilling his promise, meeting the obligations that were entered into before he ever came into office," she said. "We are providing a support-and-training mission. We will be there on the ground working with the Iraqis."

I guess she was wrong on that. Of course she will not be questioned about those statements by the media.

One can argue whether George W. Bush should have went into Iraq in the first place. When Bush left office though, thanks to the surge, Iraq was working. Even though you would never know it from the media, weapons of mass destruction, chemical weapons, were found in Iraq.

The massive cache of almost 400,000 Iraq war documents released by the WikiLeaks Web site revealed that small amounts of chemical weapons were found in Iraq and continued to surface for years after the 2003 US invasion.

The documents showed that US troops continued to find chemical weapons and labs for years after the invasion, including remnants of Saddam Hussein's chemical weapons arsenal.

In August 2004, American troops were able to buy containers from locals of what they thought was liquid sulfur mustard, a blister agent, the documents revealed. The chemicals were triple-sealed and taken to a secure site.

Also in 2004, troops discovered a chemical lab in a house in Fallujah during a battle with insurgents. A chemical cache was also found in the city.

ISIS has also used some of Iraq's chemical weapons on the Kurds. US troops were injured trying to dispose of some of the chemical weapons.

"Let's be blunt: It was a policy decision to withdraw completely from Iraq," Michael Rubin, a former Pentagon adviser on Iran and Iraq, told the Free Beacon. "Iraqis complained that Obama and Clinton simply wouldn't take 'yes' for an answer in having some Americans stay."

"The idea that the Iraqis wouldn't give American forces immunity is nonsense," Rubin explained. "The problem was that Obama and Clinton demanded the Iraqi parliament ratify such an agreement, even though constitutionally it wasn't necessary."

"Basically, what happened was a cynical political game," Rubin added. "Obama saw the Iraq war as original sin. He figured he'd withdraw completely against all advice. If Iraq went to hell, he'd blame Bush and if somehow it succeeded, he'd claim credit. That Hillary went along with this shows just how willing she is to put politics above national security and lives."

For a former Pentagon adviser for the Obama Administration to come out that bluntly and criticize them is almost unheard of. He wasn't the only one.

Former Defense Secretary Leon Panetta came out publically, and in his book, to criticize the failure to get the Status of Forces Agreement. He criticized the decision to not leave at least 8,000 troops in Iraq. He said even that number would have prevented ISIS from forming or at least growing so large. Panetta also said he felt like the American people deserved to know because of Obama's pullout, the war against ISIS will be long and drawn out.

To be fair, Bush had a problem getting a Status of Forces Agreement with Iraq also. The big difference? Bush got personally involved in the negotiation and got it done. Obama didn't want it done. He simply wanted out. Look at the loss of life because of his desires.

In fairness one cannot blame everything that has happened in Syria on Obama and Hillary. They do however share a lot of the blame. Were it not for the pullout from Iraq, ISIS would not have formed and entered the Civil War in Syria. ISIS involvement in Syria tremendously affected the Syrian Civil War. ISIS involvement in Syria gave them the financing and recruits to invade Iraq.

The pullout from Iraq, gave Iraqi Prime Minister Nouri al-Maliki the opportunity to purge many of the US trained Generals and Sunni troops from the military. They were replaced by Shia members who are more loyal to Iran. Therefore, when the Sunni based ISIS invaded from Syria, many of the Iraqi military, security, and police forces, threw down their American provided weapons, ammunition, and supplies and ran. This gave ISIS tremendous amounts of American weaponry far superior to what they had.

The oilfields and refineries captured in Syria and Iraq made ISIS the best funded terrorist group in history. When Obama finally was shamed into doing something to stop the spread of the cancer known as ISIS, he started a bombing campaign. Often American planes would return to their base with all of their missiles and bombs because they couldn't get the permission to bomb the targets they found.

For instance, they were not allowed to bomb the oilfields or refineries ISIS controlled that were funding the ISIS Jihad. Until it was finally made public, they were not even allowed to bomb the tankers carrying the oil to the market to sell! They were forced to abandon bombing large convoys of trunks on the way to Turkey loaded with oil! The public outcry was so huge they finally did start bombing the trucks, still not bombing refineries or oilfields.

Another way they facilitated the Syrian crisis was the redline statement by Obama. A President should never issue a public red line or ultimatum he or she is not prepared to enforce. That only emboldens the enemy. When Obama issued his redline then didn't follow through he emboldened America's enemies. All of them. Not just Iran and Syria.

We need to look at some other things that have happened in Iraq and Syria since the redline fiasco and the explosion of ISIS. All of which can at least be attributed to the failed policies of Obama and Hillary.

ISIS has kidnapped over 6,000 Yazidi's since their inception. Mostly women and children. There have been about 3,000 who have escaped. Most of those were women and girls who were sold and traded around as sex slaves. There are between 3,200 and 3,700 who are still captured. Most of, if not all of the men captured are feared dead. Young boys who were captured were checked for pubic hair or underarm hair. If either was present the young boy was brutally slaughter just like the men.

Of the 3,000 Yazidi women and girls who escaped, many are living in tents in refugee camps. There are approximately 1,600 of these survivors in Iraq, who are staying in tents, No one really takes care of them though. Think of a girl, woman or child, who lost everything and has been a captive more of ISI. A girl like that has no social or economic existence, no family left, and experiences so horrible you and I can't even begin to imagine.

There are verifiable reports of Mothers being fed body parts of their own children. Parents being sent their children's body parts in burlap bags. Parent's being forced to watch as their children are beheaded.

We have to remember it wasn't only Yazidi's who were treated this way. It was all Religious minorities in ISIS controlled areas. Christians, Shia Muslims, everyone. Even Sunni Muslims who don't agree with ISIS. The Kurds were even attacked with chemical weapons!

We all have seen the beheading videos released by ISIS. The videos of mass executions, the Jordanian pilot being burned alive, and the videos smuggled out of the ISIS sex slave market in Syria.

There have been an estimated 500,000 Syrian civilians killed. There are an estimated 5,000,000 refugees from Syria alone. Entire Christian communities that have existed more than 2,000 years in the same area are gone. Either as refugees, forced conversion or killed. The Vicar of Bagdad told of a story of 4 children who were captured and told by ISIS they had to convert to ISIS or be killed. The 4 children refused and were beheaded.

We have seen the videos of homosexuals being thrown from tall buildings by ISIS. Should they survive the fall, they are then stoned by the onlookers. Remember it is the very party who *claims* to support women's rights and gay rights whose policies have allowed this group to flourish.

We have been lied to by this administration about the true size and severity of ISIS. There have been rumors from well-placed sources that the administration has been adjusting the numbers through CENTCOM to release to the public to make it appear we are doing better than we are. There is an Inspector General investigation into these allegations. It will be interesting to see. As this book was getting ready for publication, I saw a report from an Independent Terrorism expert, a man I trust, that worldwide ISIS has grown to 80,000 fighters.

80,000 so called "Holy Warriors" who think it is their duty to Allah to brutally slaughter anyone who doesn't believe as they do. Since Obama and Hillary's pullout in late 2011, ISIS has grown from 0 to 80,000. 100's of thousands have lost their lives, 10's of thousands enslaved, millions have lost everything. Not Obama though. He got to fulfill his wishes, no matter the human cost. Hillary was right beside him. Neither must have a conscious or they couldn't sleep at night.

Chapter 8 - The US Constitution

I would like to explain why The Declaration of Independence, The U.S Constitution, The Amendments, and The Bill of Rights are included in this book. Just as important why they are placed before the next chapter.

In the following chapter you will read what I fell is the worst damage done to our country by Obama and Hillary. I think it is very important while reading that chapter for you to have these extremely important documents at your fingertips to refer to. I also feel it is very important for every American to have these documents. To study these documents. To protect these documents and the freedoms they guarantee.

Many Americans have sacrificed and died to defend these freedoms and pass them on to us. They have always been attacked from outside of the US, but for the past 25-30 years they have been under attack from the inside also. In the past 8 years that inside attack has escalated tremendously!

Hillary and Obama have done everything they can to skirt these documents. To change them through court actions and Executive Orders. Hillary has promised even more Executive Orders if she is elected in order to get around The Constitution.

These documents have served us well for 240 years. We must not allow any politician, Republican, Democrat, or Independent to change or violate any of these documents. As they go, so go our freedoms.

The Declaration of Independence: A Transcription

IN CONGRESS, July 4, 1776.

The unanimous Declaration of the thirteen united States of America,

When in the Course of human events, it becomes necessary for one people to dissolve the political bands which have connected them with another, and to assume among the powers of the earth, the separate and equal station to which the Laws of Nature and of Nature's God entitle them, a decent respect to the opinions of mankind requires that they should declare the causes which impel them to the separation.

We hold these truths to be self-evident, that all men are created equal, that they are endowed by their Creator with certain unalienable Rights, that among these are Life, Liberty and the pursuit of Happiness.--That to secure these rights, Governments are instituted among Men, deriving their just powers from the consent of the governed, --That whenever any Form of Government becomes destructive of these ends, it is the Right of the People to alter or to abolish it, and to institute new Government, laying its foundation on such principles and organizing its powers in such form, as to them shall seem most likely to effect their Safety and Happiness. Prudence, indeed, will dictate that Governments long established should not be changed for light and transient causes; and accordingly all experience hath shewn, that mankind are more disposed to suffer, while evils are sufferable, than to right themselves by abolishing the forms to which they are accustomed. But when a long train of abuses and usurpations, pursuing invariably the same Object evinces a design to reduce them under absolute Despotism, it is their right, it is their duty, to throw off such Government, and to provide new Guards for their future security.--Such has been the patient sufferance of these Colonies; and such is now the necessity which constrains them to alter their former Systems of Government. The history of the present King of Great Britain is a history of repeated injuries and usurpations, all having in direct object the establishment of an absolute Tyranny over these States. To prove this, let Facts be submitted to a candid world.

He has refused his Assent to Laws, the most wholesome and necessary for the public good.

He has forbidden his Governors to pass Laws of immediate and pressing importance, unless suspended in their operation till his Assent should be obtained; and when so suspended, he has utterly neglected to attend to them.

He has refused to pass other Laws for the accommodation of large districts of people, unless those people would relinquish the right of Representation in the Legislature, a right inestimable to them and formidable to tyrants only.

He has called together legislative bodies at places unusual, uncomfortable, and distant from the depository of their public Records, for the sole purpose of fatiguing them into compliance with his measures.

He has dissolved Representative Houses repeatedly, for opposing with manly firmness his invasions on the rights of the people.

He has refused for a long time, after such dissolutions, to cause others to be elected; whereby the Legislative powers, incapable of Annihilation, have returned to the

People at large for their exercise; the State remaining in the mean time exposed to all the dangers of invasion from without, and convulsions within.

He has endeavoured to prevent the population of these States; for that purpose obstructing the Laws for Naturalization of Foreigners; refusing to pass others to encourage their migrations hither, and raising the conditions of new Appropriations of Lands.

He has obstructed the Administration of Justice, by refusing his Assent to Laws for establishing Judiciary powers.

He has made Judges dependent on his Will alone, for the tenure of their offices, and the amount and payment of their salaries.

He has erected a multitude of New Offices, and sent hither swarms of Officers to harrass our people, and eat out their substance.

He has kept among us, in times of peace, Standing Armies without the Consent of our legislatures.

He has affected to render the Military independent of and superior to the Civil power.

He has combined with others to subject us to a jurisdiction foreign to our constitution, and unacknowledged by our laws; giving his Assent to their Acts of pretended Legislation:

For Quartering large bodies of armed troops among us:

For protecting them, by a mock Trial, from punishment for any Murders which they should commit on the Inhabitants of these States:

For cutting off our Trade with all parts of the world:

For imposing Taxes on us without our Consent:

For depriving us in many cases, of the benefits of Trial by Jury:

For transporting us beyond Seas to be tried for pretended offences

For abolishing the free System of English Laws in a neighbouring Province, establishing therein an Arbitrary government, and enlarging its Boundaries so as to render it at once an example and fit instrument for introducing the same absolute rule into these Colonies:

For taking away our Charters, abolishing our most valuable Laws, and altering fundamentally the Forms of our Governments:

For suspending our own Legislatures, and declaring themselves invested with power to legislate for us in all cases whatsoever.

He has abdicated Government here, by declaring us out of his Protection and waging War against us.

He has plundered our seas, ravaged our Coasts, burnt our towns, and destroyed the lives of our people.

He is at this time transporting large Armies of foreign Mercenaries to compleat the works of death, desolation and tyranny, already begun with circumstances of Cruelty & perfidy scarcely paralleled in the most barbarous ages, and totally unworthy the Head of a civilized nation.

He has constrained our fellow Citizens taken Captive on the high Seas to bear Arms against their Country, to become the executioners of their friends and Brethren, or to fall themselves by their Hands.

He has excited domestic insurrections amongst us, and has endeavoured to bring on the inhabitants of our frontiers, the merciless Indian Savages, whose known rule of warfare, is an undistinguished destruction of all ages, sexes and conditions.

In every stage of these Oppressions We have Petitioned for Redress in the most humble terms: Our repeated Petitions have been answered only by repeated injury. A Prince whose character is thus marked by every act which may define a Tyrant, is unfit to be the ruler of a free people.

Nor have We been wanting in attentions to our Brittish brethren. We have warned them from time to time of attempts by their legislature to extend an unwarrantable jurisdiction over us. We have reminded them of the circumstances of our emigration and settlement here. We have appealed to their native justice and magnanimity, and we have conjured them by the ties of our common kindred to disavow these usurpations, which, would inevitably interrupt our connections and correspondence. They too have been deaf to the voice of justice and of consanguinity. We must, therefore, acquiesce in the necessity, which denounces our Separation, and hold them, as we hold the rest of mankind, Enemies in War, in Peace Friends.

We, therefore, the Representatives of the united States of America, in General Congress, Assembled, appealing to the Supreme Judge of the world for the rectitude of our intentions, do, in the Name, and by Authority of the good People of these Colonies, solemnly publish and declare, That these United Colonies are, and of Right ought to be Free and Independent States; that they are Absolved from all Allegiance to the British Crown, and that all political connection between them and the State of Great Britain, is and ought to be totally dissolved; and that as Free and Independent States, they have full Power to levy War, conclude Peace, contract Alliances, establish Commerce, and to do all other Acts and Things which Independent States may of right do. And for the support of this Declaration, with a firm reliance on the protection of divine Providence, we mutually pledge to each other our Lives, our Fortunes and our sacred Honor

The Constitution of the United States: A Transcription

Note: The following text is a transcription of the Constitution as it was inscribed by Jacob Shallus on parchment (the document on display in the Rotunda at the National Archives Museum.) Items that are hyperlinked have since been amended or superseded. The authenticated text of the Constitution can be found on the website of the Government Printing Office.

We the People of the United States, in Order to form a more perfect Union, establish Justice, insure domestic Tranquility, provide for the common defence, promote the general Welfare, and secure the Blessings of Liberty to ourselves and our Posterity, do ordain and establish this Constitution for the United States of America.

Article. I.

Section. 1.

All legislative Powers herein granted shall be vested in a Congress of the United States, which shall consist of a Senate and House of Representatives.

Section. 2.

The House of Representatives shall be composed of Members chosen every second Year by the People of the several States, and the Electors in each State shall have the Qualifications requisite for Electors of the most numerous Branch of the State Legislature.

No Person shall be a Representative who shall not have attained to the Age of twenty five Years, and been seven Years a Citizen of the United States, and who shall not, when elected, be an Inhabitant of that State in which he shall be chosen.

Representatives and direct Taxes shall be apportioned among the several States which may be included within this Union, according to their respective Numbers, which shall be determined by adding to the whole Number of free Persons, including those bound to Service for a Term of Years, and excluding Indians not taxed, three fifths of all other Persons. The actual Enumeration shall be made within three Years after the first Meeting of the Congress of the United States, and within every subsequent Term of ten Years, in such Manner as they shall by Law direct. The Number of Representatives shall not exceed one for every thirty Thousand, but each State shall have at Least one Representative; and until such enumeration shall be made, the State of New Hampshire shall be entitled to chuse three, Massachusetts eight, Rhode-Island and Providence Plantations one, Connecticut five, New-York six, New Jersey four, Pennsylvania eight, Delaware one, Maryland six, Virginia ten, North Carolina five, South Carolina five, and Georgia three.

When vacancies happen in the Representation from any State, the Executive Authority thereof shall issue Writs of Election to fill such Vacancies.

The House of Representatives shall chuse their Speaker and other Officers; and shall have the sole Power of Impeachment.

Section. 3.

The Senate of the United States shall be composed of two Senators from each State, chosen by the Legislature thereof, for six Years; and each Senator shall have one Vote.

Immediately after they shall be assembled in Consequence of the first Election, they shall be divided as equally as may be into three Classes. The Seats of the

Senators of the first Class shall be vacated at the Expiration of the second Year, of the second Class at the Expiration of the fourth Year, and of the third Class at the Expiration of the sixth Year, so that one third may be chosen every second Year; and if Vacancies happen by Resignation, or otherwise, during the Recess of the Legislature of any State, the Executive thereof may make temporary Appointments until the next Meeting of the Legislature, which shall then fill such Vacancies.

No Person shall be a Senator who shall not have attained to the Age of thirty Years, and been nine Years a Citizen of the United States, and who shall not, when elected, be an Inhabitant of that State for which he shall be chosen.

The Vice President of the United States shall be President of the Senate, but shall have no Vote, unless they be equally divided.

The Senate shall chuse their other Officers, and also a President pro tempore, in the Absence of the Vice President, or when he shall exercise the Office of President of the United States.

The Senate shall have the sole Power to try all Impeachments. When sitting for that Purpose, they shall be on Oath or Affirmation. When the President of the

United States is tried, the Chief Justice shall preside: And no Person shall be convicted without the Concurrence of two thirds of the Members present.

Judgment in Cases of Impeachment shall not extend further than to removal from Office, and disqualification to hold and enjoy any Office of honor, Trust or Profit under the United States: but the Party convicted shall nevertheless be liable and subject to Indictment, Trial, Judgment and Punishment, according to Law.

Section. 4.

The Times, Places and Manner of holding Elections for Senators and Representatives, shall be prescribed in each State by the Legislature thereof; but the Congress may at any time by Law make or alter such Regulations, except as to the Places of chusing Senators.

The Congress shall assemble at least once in every Year, and such Meeting shall be on the first Monday in December, unless they shall by Law appoint a different Day.

Section. 5.

Each House shall be the Judge of the Elections, Returns and Qualifications of its own Members, and a Majority of each shall constitute a Quorum to do Business; but a smaller Number may adjourn from day to day, and may be authorized to compel the Attendance of absent Members, in such Manner, and under such Penalties as each House may provide.

Each House may determine the Rules of its Proceedings, punish its Members for disorderly Behaviour, and, with the Concurrence of two thirds, expel a Member.

Each House shall keep a Journal of its Proceedings, and from time to time publish the same, excepting such Parts as may in their Judgment require Secrecy; and the Yeas and Nays of the Members of either House on any question shall, at the Desire of one fifth of those Present, be entered on the Journal.

Neither House, during the Session of Congress, shall, without the Consent of the other, adjourn for more than three days, nor to any other Place than that in which the two Houses shall be sitting.

Section. 6.

The Senators and Representatives shall receive a Compensation for their Services, to be ascertained by Law, and paid out of the Treasury of the United States. They shall in all Cases, except Treason, Felony and Breach of the Peace, be privileged from Arrest during their Attendance at the Session of their respective Houses, and in going to and returning from the same; and for any Speech or Debate in either House, they shall not be questioned in any other Place.

No Senator or Representative shall, during the Time for which he was elected, be appointed to any civil Office under the Authority of the United States, which shall have been created, or the Emoluments whereof shall have been encreased during such time; and no Person holding any Office under the United States, shall be a Member of either House during his Continuance in Office.

Section. 7.

All Bills for raising Revenue shall originate in the House of Representatives; but the Senate may propose or concur with Amendments as on other Bills.

Every Bill which shall have passed the House of Representatives and the Senate, shall, before it become a Law, be presented to the President of the United States; If he approve he shall sign it, but if not he shall return it, with his Objections to that House in which it shall have originated, who shall enter the Objections at large on their Journal, and proceed to reconsider it. If after such Reconsideration two thirds of that House shall agree to pass the Bill, it shall be sent, together with the Objections, to the other House, by which it shall likewise be reconsidered, and if approved by two thirds of that House, it shall become a Law. But in all such Cases the Votes of both Houses shall be determined by yeas and Nays, and the Names of the Persons voting for and against the Bill shall be entered on the Journal of each House respectively. If any Bill shall not be returned by the President within ten Days (Sundays excepted) after it shall have been presented to him, the Same shall be a Law, in like Manner as if he had signed it, unless the Congress by their Adjournment prevent its Return, in which Case it shall not be a Law.

Every Order, Resolution, or Vote to which the Concurrence of the Senate and House of Representatives may be necessary (except on a question of Adjournment) shall be presented to the President of the United States; and before the Same shall take Effect, shall be approved by him, or being disapproved by him, shall be repassed by two thirds of the Senate and House of Representatives, according to the Rules and Limitations prescribed in the Case of a Bill.

Section. 8.

The Congress shall have Power To lay and collect Taxes, Duties, Imposts and Excises, to pay the Debts and provide for the common Defence and general Welfare of the United States; but all Duties, Imposts and Excises shall be uniform throughout the United States;

To borrow Money on the credit of the United States;

To regulate Commerce with foreign Nations, and among the several States, and with the Indian Tribes;

To establish an uniform Rule of Naturalization, and uniform Laws on the subject of Bankruptcies throughout the United States;

To coin Money, regulate the Value thereof, and of foreign Coin, and fix the Standard of Weights and Measures;

To provide for the Punishment of counterfeiting the Securities and current Coin of the United States;

To establish Post Offices and post Roads;

To promote the Progress of Science and useful Arts, by securing for limited Times to Authors and Inventors the exclusive Right to their respective Writings and Discoveries;

To constitute Tribunals inferior to the supreme Court;

To define and punish Piracies and Felonies committed on the high Seas, and Offences against the Law of Nations;

To declare War, grant Letters of Marque and Reprisal, and make Rules concerning Captures on Land and Water;

To raise and support Armies, but no Appropriation of Money to that Use shall be for a longer Term than two Years;

To provide and maintain a Navy;

To make Rules for the Government and Regulation of the land and naval Forces;

To provide for calling forth the Militia to execute the Laws of the Union, suppress Insurrections and repel Invasions;

To provide for organizing, arming, and disciplining, the Militia, and for governing such Part of them as may be employed in the Service of the United States, reserving to the States respectively, the Appointment of the Officers, and the Authority of training the Militia according to the discipline prescribed by Congress;

To exercise exclusive Legislation in all Cases whatsoever, over such District (not exceeding ten Miles square) as may, by Cession of particular States, and the Acceptance of Congress, become the Seat of the Government of the United States, and to exercise like Authority over all Places purchased by the Consent of the Legislature of the State in which the Same shall be, for the Erection of Forts, Magazines, Arsenals, dock-Yards, and other needful Buildings;—And

To make all Laws which shall be necessary and proper for carrying into Execution the foregoing Powers, and all other Powers vested by this Constitution in the Government of the United States, or in any Department or Officer thereof.

Section. 9.

The Migration or Importation of such Persons as any of the States now existing shall think proper to admit, shall not be prohibited by the Congress prior to the Year one thousand eight hundred and eight, but a Tax or duty may be imposed on such Importation, not exceeding ten dollars for each Person.

The Privilege of the Writ of Habeas Corpus shall not be suspended, unless when in Cases of Rebellion or Invasion the public Safety may require it.

No Bill of Attainder or ex post facto Law shall be passed.

No Capitation, or other direct, Tax shall be laid, unless in Proportion to the Census or enumeration herein before directed to be taken.

No Tax or Duty shall be laid on Articles exported from any State.

No Preference shall be given by any Regulation of Commerce or Revenue to the Ports of one State over those of another: nor shall Vessels bound to, or from, one State, be obliged to enter, clear, or pay Duties in another.

No Money shall be drawn from the Treasury, but in Consequence of Appropriations made by Law; and a regular Statement and Account of the Receipts and Expenditures of all public Money shall be published from time to time.

No Title of Nobility shall be granted by the United States: And no Person holding any Office of Profit or Trust under them, shall, without the Consent of the Congress, accept of any present, Emolument, Office, or Title, of any kind whatever, from any King, Prince, or foreign State.

Section. 10.

No State shall enter into any Treaty, Alliance, or Confederation; grant Letters of Marque and Reprisal; coin Money; emit Bills of Credit; make any Thing but gold and silver Coin a Tender in Payment of Debts; pass any Bill of Attainder, ex post facto Law, or Law impairing the Obligation of Contracts, or grant any Title of Nobility.

No State shall, without the Consent of the Congress, lay any Imposts or Duties on Imports or Exports, except what may be absolutely necessary for executing it's inspection Laws: and the net Produce of all Duties and Imposts, laid by any State on Imports or Exports, shall be for the Use of the Treasury of the United States; and all such Laws shall be subject to the Revision and Controul of the Congress.

No State shall, without the Consent of Congress, lay any Duty of Tonnage, keep Troops, or Ships of War in time of Peace, enter into any Agreement or Compact with another State, or with a foreign Power, or engage in War, unless actually invaded, or in such imminent Danger as will not admit of delay.

Article. II.

Section. 1.

The executive Power shall be vested in a President of the United States of America. He shall hold his Office during the Term of four Years, and, together with the Vice President, chosen for the same Term, be elected, as follows

Each State shall appoint, in such Manner as the Legislature thereof may direct, a Number of Electors, equal to the whole Number of Senators and Representatives to which the State may be entitled in the Congress: but no Senator or Representative, or Person holding an Office of Trust or Profit under the United States, shall be appointed an Elector.

The Electors shall meet in their respective States, and vote by Ballot for two Persons, of whom one at least shall not be an Inhabitant of the same State with themselves. And they shall make a List of all the Persons voted for, and of the Number of Votes for each; which List they shall sign and certify, and transmit sealed to the Seat of the Government of the United States, directed to the President of the Senate. The President of the Senate shall, in the Presence of the Senate and House of Representatives, open all the Certificates, and the Votes shall then be counted. The Person having the greatest Number of Votes shall be the President, if such Number be a Majority of the whole Number of Electors appointed; and if there be more than one who have such Majority, and have an equal Number of Votes, then the House of Representatives shall immediately chuse by Ballot one of them for President; and if no Person have a Majority, then from the five highest on the List the said House shall in like Manner chuse the President. But in chusing the President, the Votes shall be taken by States, the Representation from each State having one Vote; A quorum for this Purpose shall consist of a Member or Members from two thirds of the States, and a Majority of all the States shall be necessary to a Choice. In every Case, after the Choice of the President, the Person having the greatest Number of Votes of the Electors shall be the Vice President. But if there should remain two or more who have equal Votes, the Senate shall chuse from them by Ballot the Vice President.

The Congress may determine the Time of chusing the Electors, and the Day on which they shall give their Votes; which Day shall be the same throughout the United States.

No Person except a natural born Citizen, or a Citizen of the United States, at the time of the Adoption of this Constitution, shall be eligible to the Office of President; neither shall any Person be eligible to that Office who shall not have attained to the Age of thirty five Years, and been fourteen Years a Resident within the United States.

In Case of the Removal of the President from Office, or of his Death, Resignation, or Inability to discharge the Powers and Duties of the said Office, the Same shall devolve on the Vice President, and the Congress may by Law provide for the Case of Removal, Death,

Resignation or Inability, both of the President and Vice President, declaring what Officer shall then act as President, and such Officer shall act accordingly, until the Disability be removed, or a President shall be elected.

The President shall, at stated Times, receive for his Services, a Compensation, which shall neither be encreased nor diminished during the Period for which he shall have been elected, and he shall not receive within that Period any other Emolument from the United States, or any of them.

Before he enter on the Execution of his Office, he shall take the following Oath or Affirmation:—"I do solemnly swear (or affirm) that I will faithfully execute the Office of President of the United States, and will to the best of my Ability, preserve, protect and defend the Constitution of the United States."

Section. 2.

The President shall be Commander in Chief of the Army and Navy of the United States, and of the Militia of the several States, when called into the actual Service of the United States; he may require the Opinion, in writing, of the principal Officer in each of the executive Departments, upon any Subject relating to the Duties of their respective Offices, and he shall have Power to grant Reprieves and Pardons for Offences against the United States, except in Cases of Impeachment.

He shall have Power, by and with the Advice and Consent of the Senate, to make Treaties, provided two thirds of the Senators present concur; and he shall nominate, and by and with the Advice and Consent of the Senate, shall appoint Ambassadors, other public Ministers and Consuls, Judges of the supreme Court, and all other Officers of the United States, whose Appointments are not herein otherwise provided for, and which shall be established by Law: but the Congress may by Law vest the Appointment of such inferior Officers, as they think proper, in the President alone, in the Courts of Law, or in the Heads of Departments.

The President shall have Power to fill up all Vacancies that may happen during the Recess of the Senate, by granting Commissions which shall expire at the End of their next Session.

Section. 3.

He shall from time to time give to the Congress Information of the State of the Union, and recommend to their Consideration such Measures as he shall judge necessary and expedient; he may, on extraordinary Occasions, convene both Houses, or either of them, and in Case of Disagreement between them, with Respect to the Time of Adjournment, he may adjourn them to such Time as he shall think proper; he shall receive Ambassadors and other public Ministers; he shall take Care that the Laws be faithfully executed, and shall Commission all the Officers of the United States.

Section. 4.

The President, Vice President and all civil Officers of the United States, shall be removed from Office on Impeachment for, and Conviction of, Treason, Bribery, or other high Crimes and Misdemeanors.

Article III.

Section. 1.

The judicial Power of the United States, shall be vested in one supreme Court, and in such inferior Courts as the Congress may from time to time ordain and establish. The Judges, both of the supreme and inferior Courts, shall hold their Offices during good Behaviour, and shall, at stated Times, receive for their Services, a Compensation, which shall not be diminished during their Continuance in Office.

Section. 2.

The judicial Power shall extend to all Cases, in Law and Equity, arising under this Constitution, the Laws of the United States, and Treaties made, or which shall be made, under their Authority;—to all Cases affecting Ambassadors, other public Ministers and Consuls;—to all Cases of admiralty and maritime Jurisdiction;—to Controversies to which the United States shall be a Party;—to Controversies between two or more States;—between a State and Citizens of another State,—between Citizens of different States,—between Citizens of the same State claiming Lands under Grants of different States, and between a State, or the Citizens thereof, and foreign States, Citizens or Subjects.

In all Cases affecting Ambassadors, other public Ministers and Consuls, and those in which a State shall be Party, the supreme Court shall have original Jurisdiction. In all the other Cases before mentioned, the supreme Court shall have appellate Jurisdiction, both as to Law and Fact, with such Exceptions, and under such Regulations as the Congress shall make.

The Trial of all Crimes, except in Cases of Impeachment, shall be by Jury; and such Trial shall be held in the State where the said Crimes shall have been committed; but when not committed within any State, the Trial shall be at such Place or Places as the Congress may by Law have directed.

Section. 3.

Treason against the United States, shall consist only in levying War against them, or in adhering to their Enemies, giving them Aid and Comfort. No Person shall be convicted of Treason unless on the Testimony of two Witnesses to the same overt Act, or on Confession in open Court.

The Congress shall have Power to declare the Punishment of Treason, but no Attainder of Treason shall work Corruption of Blood, or Forfeiture except during the Life of the Person attainted.

Article. IV.

Section. 1.

Full Faith and Credit shall be given in each State to the public Acts, Records, and judicial Proceedings of every other State. And the Congress may by general Laws prescribe the Manner in which such Acts, Records and Proceedings shall be proved, and the Effect thereof.

Section. 2.

The Citizens of each State shall be entitled to all Privileges and Immunities of Citizens in the several States.

A Person charged in any State with Treason, Felony, or other Crime, who shall flee from Justice, and be found in another State, shall on Demand of the executive Authority of the State from which he fled, be delivered up, to be removed to the State having Jurisdiction of the Crime.

No Person held to Service or Labour in one State, under the Laws thereof, escaping into another, shall, in Consequence of any Law or Regulation therein, be discharged from such Service or Labour, but shall be delivered up on Claim of the Party to whom such Service or Labour may be due.

Section. 3.

New States may be admitted by the Congress into this Union; but no new State shall be formed or erected within the Jurisdiction of any other State; nor any State be formed by the Junction of two or more States, or Parts of States, without the Consent of the Legislatures of the States concerned as well as of the Congress.

The Congress shall have Power to dispose of and make all needful Rules and Regulations respecting the Territory or other Property belonging to the United States; and nothing in this Constitution shall be so construed as to Prejudice any Claims of the United States, or of any particular State.

Section. 4.

The United States shall guarantee to every State in this Union a Republican Form of Government, and shall protect each of them against Invasion; and on Application of the Legislature, or of the Executive (when the Legislature cannot be convened), against domestic Violence.

Article. V.

The Congress, whenever two thirds of both Houses shall deem it necessary, shall propose Amendments to this Constitution, or, on the Application of the Legislatures of two thirds of the several States, shall call a Convention for proposing Amendments, which, in either Case, shall be valid to all Intents and Purposes, as Part of this Constitution, when ratified by the Legislatures of three fourths of the several States, or by Conventions in three fourths thereof, as the one or the other Mode of Ratification may be proposed by the Congress; Provided that no Amendment which may be made prior to the Year One thousand eight hundred and eight shall in any Manner affect the first and fourth Clauses in the Ninth Section of the first Article; and that no State, without its Consent, shall be deprived of its equal Suffrage in the Senate.

Article. VI.

All Debts contracted and Engagements entered into, before the Adoption of this Constitution, shall be as valid against the United States under this Constitution, as under the Confederation.

This Constitution, and the Laws of the United States which shall be made in Pursuance thereof; and all Treaties made, or which shall be made, under the Authority of the United States, shall be the supreme Law of the Land; and the Judges in every State shall be bound thereby, any Thing in the Constitution or Laws of any State to the Contrary notwithstanding.

The Senators and Representatives before mentioned, and the Members of the several State Legislatures, and all executive and judicial Officers, both of the United States and of the several States, shall be bound by Oath or Affirmation, to support this Constitution; but no religious Test shall ever be required as a Qualification to any Office or public Trust under the United States.

Article. VII.

The Ratification of the Conventions of nine States, shall be sufficient for the Establishment of this Constitution between the States so ratifying the Same.

The Word, "the," being interlined between the seventh and eighth Lines of the first Page, The Word "Thirty" being partly written on an Erazure in the fifteenth Line of the first Page, The Words "is tried" being interlined between the thirty second and thirty third Lines of the first Page and the Word "the" being interlined between the forty third and forty fourth Lines of the second Page.

Attest William Jackson Secretary

done in Convention by the Unanimous Consent of the States present the Seventeenth Day of September in the Year of our Lord one thousand seven hundred and Eighty seven and of the Independance of the United States of America the Twelfth In witness whereof We have hereunto subscribed our Names,

The U.S. Bill of Rights

The Preamble to The Bill of Rights

Congress of the United States

begun and held at the City of New-York, on

Wednesday the fourth of March, one thousand seven hundred and eighty nine.

THE Conventions of a number of the States, having at the time of their adopting the Constitution, expressed a desire, in order to prevent misconstruction or abuse of its powers, that further declaratory and restrictive clauses should be added: And as extending the ground of public confidence in the Government, will best ensure the beneficent ends of its institution.

RESOLVED by the Senate and House of Representatives of the United States of America, in Congress assembled, two thirds of both Houses concurring, that the following Articles be proposed to the Legislatures of the several States, as amendments to the Constitution of the United States, all, or any of which Articles, when ratified by three fourths of the said Legislatures, to be valid to all intents and purposes, as part of the said Constitution; viz.

ARTICLES in addition to, and Amendment of the Constitution of the United States of America, proposed by Congress, and ratified by the Legislatures of the several States, pursuant to the fifth Article of the original Constitution.

Note: The following text is a transcription of the first ten amendments to the Constitution in their original form. These amendments were ratified December 15, 1791, and form what is known as the "Bill of Rights."

Amendment I

Congress shall make no law respecting an establishment of religion, or prohibiting the free exercise thereof; or abridging the freedom of speech, or of the press; or the right of the people peaceably to assemble, and to petition the Government for a redress of grievances.

Amendment II

A well regulated Militia, being necessary to the security of a free State, the right of the people to keep and bear Arms, shall not be infringed.

Amendment III

No Soldier shall, in time of peace be quartered in any house, without the consent of the Owner, nor in time of war, but in a manner to be prescribed by law.

Amendment IV

The right of the people to be secure in their persons, houses, papers, and effects, against unreasonable searches and seizures, shall not be violated, and no Warrants shall issue, but upon probable cause, supported by Oath or affirmation, and particularly describing the place to be searched, and the persons or things to be seized.

Amendment V

No person shall be held to answer for a capital, or otherwise infamous crime, unless on a presentment or indictment of a Grand Jury, except in cases arising in the land or naval forces, or in the Militia, when in actual service in time of War or public danger; nor shall any person be subject for the same offence to be twice put in jeopardy of life or limb; nor shall be compelled in any criminal case to be a witness against himself, nor be deprived of life, liberty, or property, without due process of law; nor shall private property be taken for public use, without just compensation.

Amendment VI

In all criminal prosecutions, the accused shall enjoy the right to a speedy and public trial, by an impartial jury of the State and district wherein the crime shall have been committed, which district shall have been previously ascertained by law, and to be informed of the nature and cause of the accusation; to be confronted with the witnesses against him; to have compulsory process for obtaining witnesses in his favor, and to have the Assistance of Counsel for his defence.

Amendment VII

In Suits at common law, where the value in controversy shall exceed twenty dollars, the right of trial by jury shall be preserved, and no fact tried by a jury, shall be otherwise re-examined in any Court of the United States, than according to the rules of the common law.

Amendment VIII

Excessive bail shall not be required, nor excessive fines imposed, nor cruel and unusual punishments inflicted.

Amendment IX

The enumeration in the Constitution, of certain rights, shall not be construed to deny or disparage others retained by the people.

Amendment X

The powers not delegated to the United States by the Constitution, nor prohibited by it to the States, are reserved to the States respectively, or to the people.

The Constitution: Amendments 11-27

Constitutional Amendments 1-10 make up what is known as The Bill of Rights.

Amendments 11-27 are listed below.

AMENDMENT XI

Passed by Congress March 4, 1794. Ratified February 7, 1795.

Note: Article III, section 2, of the Constitution was modified by amendment 11.

The Judicial power of the United States shall not be construed to extend to any suit in law or equity, commenced or prosecuted against one of the United States by Citizens of another State, or by Citizens or Subjects of any Foreign State.

AMENDMENT XII

Passed by Congress December 9, 1803. Ratified June 15, 1804.

Note: A portion of Article II, section 1 of the
Constitution was superseded by the 12th amendment.

The Electors shall meet in their respective states and vote
by ballot for President and Vice-President, one of whom,
at least, shall not be an inhabitant of the same state with
themselves; they shall name in their ballots the person
voted for as President, and in distinct ballots the person
voted for as Vice-President, and they shall make distinct
lists of all persons voted for as President, and of all
persons voted for as Vice-President, and of the number of
votes for each, which lists they shall sign and certify, and
transmit sealed to the seat of the government of the
United States, directed to the President of the Senate; --
the President of the Senate shall, in the presence of the
Senate and House of Representatives, open all the
certificates and the votes shall then be counted; -- The
person having the greatest number of votes for President,
shall be the President, if such number be a majority of the
whole number of Electors appointed; and if no person
have such majority, then from the persons having the
highest numbers not exceeding three on the list of those
voted for as President, the House of Representatives shall
choose immediately, by ballot, the President. But in
choosing the President, the votes shall be taken by states,
the representation from each state having one vote; a
quorum for this purpose shall consist of a member or
members from two-thirds of the states, and a majority of
all the states shall be necessary to a choice. [And if the
House of Representatives shall not choose a President

whenever the right of choice shall devolve upon them, before the fourth day of March next following, then the Vice-President shall act as President, as in case of the death or other constitutional disability of the President. --]* The person having the greatest number of votes as Vice-President, shall be the Vice-President, if such number be a majority of the whole number of Electors appointed, and if no person have a majority, then from the two highest numbers on the list, the Senate shall choose the Vice-President; a quorum for the purpose shall consist of two-thirds of the whole number of Senators, and a majority of the whole number shall be necessary to a choice. But no person constitutionally ineligible to the office of President shall be eligible to that of Vice-President of the United States.

*Superseded by section 3 of the 20th amendment.

AMENDMENT XIII

Passed by Congress January 31, 1865. Ratified December 6, 1865.

Note: A portion of Article IV, section 2, of the Constitution was superseded by the 13th amendment.

Section 1.

Neither slavery nor involuntary servitude, except as a punishment for crime whereof the party shall have been duly convicted, shall exist within the United States, or any place subject to their jurisdiction.

Section 2.

Congress shall have power to enforce this article by appropriate legislation.

AMENDMENT XIV

Passed by Congress June 13, 1866. Ratified July 9, 1868.

Note: Article I, section 2, of the Constitution was modified by section 2 of the 14th amendment.

Section 1.

All persons born or naturalized in the United States, and subject to the jurisdiction thereof, are citizens of the United States and of the State wherein they reside. No State shall make or enforce any law which shall abridge the privileges or immunities of citizens of the United States; nor shall any State deprive any person of life, liberty, or property, without due process of law; nor deny to any person within its jurisdiction the equal protection of the laws.

Section 2.

Representatives shall be apportioned among the several States according to their respective numbers, counting the whole number of persons in each State, excluding Indians not taxed. But when the right to vote at any election for the choice of electors for President and Vice-President of the United States, Representatives in Congress, the Executive and Judicial officers of a State, or the members of the Legislature thereof, is denied to any of the male inhabitants of such State, being twenty-one years of age,* and citizens of the United States, or in any way abridged, except for participation in rebellion, or other crime, the basis of representation therein shall be reduced in the proportion which the number of such male citizens shall bear to the whole number of male citizens twenty-one years of age in such State.

Section 3.

No person shall be a Senator or Representative in Congress, or elector of President and Vice-President, or hold any office, civil or military, under the United States, or under any State, who, having previously taken an oath, as a member of Congress, or as an officer of the United States, or as a member of any State legislature, or as an executive or judicial officer of any State, to support the Constitution of the United States, shall have engaged in insurrection or rebellion against the same, or given aid or comfort to the enemies thereof. But Congress may by a vote of two-thirds of each House, remove such disability.

Section 4.

The validity of the public debt of the United States, authorized by law, including debts incurred for payment of pensions and bounties for services in suppressing insurrection or rebellion, shall not be questioned. But neither the United States nor any State shall assume or pay any debt or obligation incurred in aid of insurrection or rebellion against the United States, or any claim for the loss or emancipation of any slave; but all such debts, obligations and claims shall be held illegal and void.

Section 5.

The Congress shall have the power to enforce, by appropriate legislation, the provisions of this article.

*Changed by section 1 of the 26th amendment.

AMENDMENT XV

Passed by Congress February 26, 1869. Ratified February 3, 1870.

Section 1.

The right of citizens of the United States to vote shall not be denied or abridged by the United States or by any State on account of race, color, or previous condition of servitude--

Section 2.

The Congress shall have the power to enforce this article by appropriate legislation.

AMENDMENT XVI

Passed by Congress July 2, 1909. Ratified February 3, 1913.

Note: Article I, section 9, of the Constitution was modified by amendment 16.

The Congress shall have power to lay and collect taxes on incomes, from whatever source derived, without apportionment among the several States, and without regard to any census or enumeration.

AMENDMENT XVII

Passed by Congress May 13, 1912. Ratified April 8, 1913.

Note: Article I, section 3, of the Constitution was modified by the 17th amendment.

The Senate of the United States shall be composed of two Senators from each State, elected by the people thereof, for six years; and each Senator shall have one vote. The electors in each State shall have the qualifications requisite for electors of the most numerous branch of the State legislatures.

When vacancies happen in the representation of any State in the Senate, the executive authority of such State shall issue writs of election to fill such vacancies: Provided, That the legislature of any State may empower the executive thereof to make temporary appointments until the people fill the vacancies by election as the legislature may direct.

This amendment shall not be so construed as to affect the election or term of any Senator chosen before it becomes valid as part of the Constitution.

AMENDMENT XVIII

Passed by Congress December 18, 1917. Ratified January 16, 1919. Repealed by amendment 21.

Section 1.

 After one year from the ratification of this article the manufacture, sale, or transportation of intoxicating liquors within, the importation thereof into, or the exportation thereof from the United States and all territory subject to the jurisdiction thereof for beverage purposes is hereby prohibited.

Section 2.

The Congress and the several States shall have concurrent power to enforce this article by appropriate legislation.

Section 3.

This article shall be inoperative unless it shall have been ratified as an amendment to the Constitution by the legislatures of the several States, as provided in the Constitution, within seven years from the date of the submission hereof to the States by the Congress.

AMENDMENT XIX

Passed by Congress June 4, 1919. Ratified August 18, 1920.

The right of citizens of the United States to vote shall not be denied or abridged by the United States or by any State on account of sex.

Congress shall have power to enforce this article by appropriate legislation.

AMENDMENT XX

Passed by Congress March 2, 1932. Ratified January 23, 1933.

Note: Article I, section 4, of the Constitution was modified by section 2 of this amendment. In addition, a portion of the 12th amendment was superseded by section 3.

Section 1.

The terms of the President and the Vice President shall end at noon on the 20th day of January, and the terms of Senators and Representatives at noon on the 3d day of January, of the years in which such terms would have ended if this article had not been ratified; and the terms of their successors shall then begin.

Section 2.

The Congress shall assemble at least once in every year, and such meeting shall begin at noon on the 3d day of January, unless they shall by law appoint a different day.

Section 3.

If, at the time fixed for the beginning of the term of the President, the President elect shall have died, the Vice President elect shall become President. If a President shall not have been chosen before the time fixed for the beginning of his term, or if the President elect shall have failed to qualify, then the Vice President elect shall act as President until a President shall have qualified; and the Congress may by law provide for the case wherein neither a President elect nor a Vice President elect shall have qualified, declaring who shall then act as President, or the manner in which one who is to act shall be selected, and such person shall act accordingly until a President or Vice President shall have qualified.

Section 4.

The Congress may by law provide for the case of the death of any of the persons from whom the House of Representatives may choose a President whenever the right of choice shall have devolved upon them, and for the case of the death of any of the persons from whom the Senate may choose a Vice President whenever the right of choice shall have devolved upon them.

Section 5.

Sections 1 and 2 shall take effect on the 15th day of October following the ratification of this article.

Section 6.

This article shall be inoperative unless it shall have been ratified as an amendment to the Constitution by the legislatures of three-fourths of the several States within seven years from the date of its submission.

AMENDMENT XXI

Passed by Congress February 20, 1933. Ratified December 5, 1933.

Section 1.

The eighteenth article of amendment to the Constitution of the United States is hereby repealed.

Section 2.

The transportation or importation into any State, Territory, or possession of the United States for delivery or use therein of intoxicating liquors, in violation of the laws thereof, is hereby prohibited.

Section 3.

This article shall be inoperative unless it shall have been ratified as an amendment to the Constitution by conventions in the several States, as provided in the Constitution, within seven years from the date of the submission hereof to the States by the Congress.

AMENDMENT XXII

Passed by Congress March 21, 1947. Ratified February 27, 1951.

Section 1.

No person shall be elected to the office of the President more than twice, and no person who has held the office of President, or acted as President, for more than two years of a term to which some other person was elected President shall be elected to the office of the President more than once. But this Article shall not apply to any person holding the office of President when this Article was proposed by the Congress, and shall not prevent any person who may be holding the office of President, or acting as President, during the term within which this Article becomes operative from holding the office of President or acting as President during the remainder of such term.

Section 2.

This article shall be inoperative unless it shall have been ratified as an amendment to the Constitution by the legislatures of three-fourths of the several States within seven years from the date of its submission to the States by the Congress.

AMENDMENT XXIII

Passed by Congress June 16, 1960. Ratified March 29, 1961.

Section 1.

The District constituting the seat of Government of the United States shall appoint in such manner as the Congress may direct:

A number of electors of President and Vice President equal to the whole number of Senators and Representatives in Congress to which the District would be entitled if it were a State, but in no event more than the least populous State; they shall be in addition to those appointed by the States, but they shall be considered, for the purposes of the election of President and Vice President, to be electors appointed by a State; and they shall meet in the District and perform such duties as provided by the twelfth article of amendment.

Section 2.

The Congress shall have power to enforce this article by appropriate legislation.

AMENDMENT XXIV

Passed by Congress August 27, 1962. Ratified January 23, 1964.

Section 1.

The right of citizens of the United States to vote in any primary or other election for President or Vice President, for electors for President or Vice President, or for Senator or Representative in Congress, shall not be denied or abridged by the United States or any State by reason of failure to pay any poll tax or other tax.

Section 2.

The Congress shall have power to enforce this article by appropriate legislation.

AMENDMENT XXV

Passed by Congress July 6, 1965. Ratified February 10, 1967.

Note: Article II, section 1, of the Constitution was affected by the 25th amendment.

Section 1.

In case of the removal of the President from office or of his death or resignation, the Vice President shall become President.

Section 2.

Whenever there is a vacancy in the office of the Vice President, the President shall nominate a Vice President who shall take office upon confirmation by a majority vote of both Houses of Congress.

Section 3.

Whenever the President transmits to the President pro tempore of the Senate and the Speaker of the House of Representatives his written declaration that he is unable to discharge the powers and duties of his office, and until he transmits to them a written declaration to the contrary, such powers and duties shall be discharged by the Vice President as Acting President.

Section 4.

Whenever the Vice President and a majority of either the principal officers of the executive departments or of such other body as Congress may by law provide, transmit to the President pro tempore of the Senate and the Speaker of the House of Representatives their written declaration that the President is unable to discharge the powers and duties of his office, the Vice President shall immediately assume the powers and duties of the office as Acting President.

Thereafter, when the President transmits to the President pro tempore of the Senate and the Speaker of the House of Representatives his written declaration that no inability exists, he shall resume the powers and duties of his office unless the Vice President and a majority of either the principal officers of the executive department or of such other body as Congress may by law provide, transmit within four days to the President pro tempore of the Senate and the Speaker of the House of Representatives their written declaration that the President is unable to discharge the powers and duties of his office. Thereupon Congress shall decide the issue, assembling within forty-eight hours for that purpose if not in session. If the Congress, within twenty-one days after receipt of the latter written declaration, or, if Congress is not in session, within twenty-one days after Congress is required to assemble, determines by two-thirds vote of both Houses that the President is unable to discharge the powers and duties of his office, the Vice President shall continue to discharge the same as Acting President; otherwise, the President shall resume the powers and duties of his office.

AMENDMENT XXVI

Passed by Congress March 23, 1971. Ratified July 1, 1971.

Note: Amendment 14, section 2, of the Constitution was modified by section 1 of the 26th amendment.

Section 1.

The right of citizens of the United States, who are eighteen years of age or older, to vote shall not be denied or abridged by the United States or by any State on account of age.

Section 2.

The Congress shall have power to enforce this article by appropriate legislation.

AMENDMENT XXVII

Originally proposed Sept. 25, 1789. Ratified May 7, 1992.

No law, varying the compensation for the services of the Senators and Representatives, shall take effect, until an election of Representatives shall have intervened.

Chapter 9 - Immigration, More Lies, and Ethics Violations

The concept that it is permissible to lie in order to achieve your goals has gone through this entire Administration like a bad virus. Had common Americans been caught in these lies they would now reside in prison. I am going to include a partial court order, I won't bore you with the entire order. This is an example of Justice Department Attorneys lying to a Federal Judge in open court about one of Obama's illegal Executive Orders:

Case 1:14-cv-00254 Document 347 Filed in TXSD on 05/19/16 Page 2 of 28

3

As the parties know, this Court has been deliberating for quite some time about the proper way to address the series of misrepresentations made by the attorneys from the Justice Department to the

Plaintiff States and to this Court. This Court in at least one prior order has detailed the multiple times

attorneys for the Government misrepresented the actions being taken (or, according to their

representations, not being taken) by their clients. See, e.g., Doc. No. 226. These misrepresentations will

be discussed in more detail below; but suffice it to say the Government's attorneys effectively misled the

Plaintiff States into foregoing a request for a temporary restraining order or an earlier injunction hearing.

Further, these misrepresentations may have caused more damage in the intervening time period and may

cause additional damage in the future. Counsel's misrepresentations also misdirected the Court as to the

timeline involved in the implementation of the 2014 DHS Directive, which included the amendments to

the Deferred Action for Childhood Arrivals ("DACA") program.

I. The Timing of this Order

Initially, this Court had decided to postpone ruling on this matter until after a final ruling on the

merits since the injunction it entered was interlocutory, and the Court could not reasonably foresee a fact scenario in which the case would not ultimately be remanded for further proceedings. Subsequent

events have changed the landscape in this regard. Usually, the legal issues in a case narrow on appeal

until a case reaches the highest rung on the appellate ladder, at which point that court (be it a Court of

Appeals or the Supreme Court) has one or two overriding issues that it must resolve. In addressing the

request for a temporary injunction, this Court ruled, as is the custom and tradition in American

jurisprudence, on the narrowest issue that would resolve the existing controversy: the procedural issue

premises of the rule of law. When such transgressions are acknowledged yet forgiven by the courts, we endorse and invite their repetition. United States v. Olsen, 737 F.3d 625, 632 (9th Cir. 2013) (Kozinski, J., dissenting from denial of petition for rehearing en banc). Four judges joined this dissent.

4

concerning the Administrative Procedure Act ("APA"). This Court anticipated that the two issues on appeal would be this Court's ruling on standing and the procedural APA issue, with only the former

possibly being case-determinative.

This case, however, has not followed the normal progression. Instead of the issues narrowing on

appeal, they have expanded. The Fifth Circuit expanded the holding by not only affirming on the APA

procedural violation, but also by ruling that the Plaintiff States have established a substantial likelihood

of success on the merits of their claim that Defendants' actions violated substantive APA standards as

well. Texas v. United States, 809 F.3d 134, 146 (5th Cir. 2015). The Supreme Court has apparently

expanded the scope of review even further. It has not only granted review of the Fifth Circuit's judgment, but has also asked the parties to brief the constitutional issues.4 United States v. Texas, 136 S.

Ct. 906 (2016) (No. 15-674). Consequently, one now has reason to speculate that the Supreme Court

could rule in a way that would negate the need for a remand to this Court. That being the case, the most

efficacious path for this Court to follow is to proceed to rule upon what may be the only remaining issue.

II. The Misconduct Involving the Implementation of the 2014 DHS Directive

This Court has previously described the events that occurred in this case in its April 7, 2015,

order. [Doc. No. 226]. In summary, this Court and opposing counsel were misled both in writing and in

open court on multiple occasions as to when the Defendants would begin to implement the Secretary's

2014 DHS Directive establishing the Deferred Action for Parents of Americans and Lawful Permanent

Residents ("DAPA") program and amending the DACA program. Opposing counsel and this Court

were assured that no action would be taken implementing the 2014 DHS Directive until February 18,

4 This Court has not been the only observer to note this expansion on appeal. "A rather unusual aspect of the case was that, although the lower courts had not decided a constitutional question the states had raised, the Justices added that question on their own." Lyle Denniston, Immigration Policy: Review and Decision This Term, SCOTUSBLOG (Jan. 19, 2016 9:50 AM), http://scotusblog.com/2016/01/immigration-policy-review-and-decision-this-term.

Case 1:14-cv-00254 Document 347 Filed in TXSD on 05/19/16 Page 4 of 28

5

2015. Counsel for the Government made these assurances on the record on December 19, 2014, and in

open court on January 15, 2015. Similar misrepresentations were made in pleadings filed on January 14,

2015, [Doc. No. 90 at 3] and even after the injunction issued, on February 23, 2015. [Doc. No. 150].

For example, on February 23, 2015, the Government lawyers wrote that: "DHS was to begin accepting requests for modified DACA on February 18, 2015."5 [Doc. No. 150 at 7]. This representation was

made despite the fact that in actuality the DHS had already granted or renewed over 100,000 modified

DACA applications using the 2014 DHS Directive.

 At the time of the Court's April 2015 order, the Government had not filed its brief explaining its

conduct to the Court. Prior to reviewing that brief, the Court entertained a variety of possible

explanations concerning the conduct of the Government lawyers. These included the more innocuous

possibilities that the DOJ lawyers lacked knowledge or that they made an innocent mistake that led to

the misrepresentations.

Now, however, having studied the Government's filings in this case, its admissions make one conclusion indisputably clear: the Justice Department lawyers knew the true facts and misrepresented those facts to the citizens of the 26 Plaintiff States, their lawyers and this Court on multiple occasions.6

A. The Government's

The Government claims that the reason its lawyers were not candid with the Court was that they

either "lost focus on the fact" or that somehow "the fact receded in memory or awareness." [Doc. No.

242 at 18]. The Government's brief admits that its lawyers, including the lawyers who appeared in this

Court, knew that the Defendants were granting three-year DACA renewals using the three-year period

5 This date matches the Government's earlier representation that "U.S. Citizenship and Immigration Services (USCIS) does not intend to entertain requests for deferred action under the challenged policy until February 18, 2015 and even after it starts accepting requests, it will not be in a position to make any final decisions on those requests at least until March 4, 2015." [Doc. No. 90 at 3] (emphasis in the original). In reality, by March 3, 2015, over 100,000 requests had been granted. 6 "As of early December 2014, the attorneys who appeared before this Court (and many other attorneys at both the DOJ and DHS) had been informed that DHS was providing three-year deferrals to new and renewal applicants. . . ." [Doc. No. 242 at 8]. Three-year deferrals could only have been

granted using the 2014 DHS Directive. See the Government's brief quoted infra p. 7.

6

created by the 2014 DHS Directive at issue in this case. Yet the Government's lawyers chose not to tell

the Plaintiff States or the Court. In fact, the Justice Department knew that DHS was implementing the

three-year renewal portion of the 2014 DHS Directive weeks before its attorneys told this Court for the

very first time that no such action was being taken. Apparently, lawyers, somewhere in the halls of the

Justice Department whose identities are unknown to this Court, decided unilaterally that the conduct of

the DHS in granting three-year DACA renewals using the 2014 DHS Directive was immaterial and

irrelevant to this lawsuit and that the DOJ could therefore just ignore it. [Doc. No. 242 at 17]. Then, for

whatever reason, the Justice Department trial lawyers appearing in this Court chose not to tell

about this DHS activity. The first decision was certainly unsupportable, but the subsequent decision to

hide it from the Court was unethical. Such conduct is certainly not worthy of any department whose name includes the word "Justice."7 Suffice it to say, the citizens of all fifty states, their counsel, the affected aliens and the

judiciary all deserve better.

B. The Misrepresentations by the Government's Attorneys

 The Government has admitted to the Court in multiple places that both DHS and DOJ personnel

knew since November of 2014 that three-year DACA renewals were being granted. It was impossible to

grant a three-year deferral using the 2012 DACA criteria. The Government admits the only way these

three-year deferrals could be granted was pursuant to the 2014 DHS Directive—the very subject of the

States' injunction lawsuit:

7 Just recently, the Sixth Circuit expressed a similar conclusion. It wrote: In closing, we echo the district court's observations about this case. The lawyers in the Department of Justice have a long and storied tradition of defending the nation's interests and enforcing its laws—all of them, not just selective ones—in a manner worthy of the Department's nameThe conduct of the IRS's attorneys in the district court [like the attorneys representing the DHS in this Court] falls outside that tradition. We expect that the IRS will do better going forward. And we order that the IRS comply with the district court's discovery orders of April

1 and June 16, 2015—without redactions, and without further delay. In re United States, No. 15-3793, 2016 WL 1105077, at *11 (6th Cir. Mar. 22, 2016) (emphasis added). The district court had earlier written that it questioned "whether or not the Department of Justice is doing justice." Id. at *5.

Case 1:14-cv-00254 Document 347 Filed in TXSD on 05/19/16 Page 6 of 28

7

The Government does not dispute, and indeed has never disputed, that the three-year deferrals were pursuant to the 2014 Deferred Action Guidance. Likewise, there is no dispute that the Government also understood the change from two- to three-year grants of deferred action to be a contested issue in the case.

[Doc. No. 242 at 15 n.2] (citation omitted).

1. The December 2014 Misrepresentation

From day one, the Plaintiffs sought to enjoin the entire 2014 DHS Directive. [Doc. Nos. 1 & 5].

The injunction proposed by the Plaintiff States sought to prevent the implementation of "the DHS

Directive of November 20, 2014." [Doc. No. 5-1]. This by definition included the three-year DACA

deferrals. It is important to remember that the Plaintiff States initially requested that a hearing on the merits of their motion be held before December 31, 2014. [Doc. No. 5 at 12]. The Plaintiff States

agreed to a later hearing date as a result of the Government's representations made in a conference call

with the Court on December 19, 2014. During that call, counsel for the Plaintiff States agreed to a

January hearing date, but only did so after being assured by the Government that nothing would happen

between the December 19th call and the hearing date. Out of an abundance of caution, counsel had the

following exchange:

PLAINTIFF STATES' COUNSEL: . . . [W]e have been operating under the assumption . . . that we absolutely protected our interests in this and that there won't be any curve balls or surprises about, you know, deferred action documents being issued, you know, tomorrow or on the first of the year . . . [W]e have filed in our pleadings and have pointed out, that, you know, the United States has hired a thousand employees in the initial large processing center and that there are, you know, there is a potential for I think for prejudice or at least changing the calculus on the preliminary injunction inquiry if the state of the playing field changes between now and the 9th of January.

THE COURT: . . . [D]o you anticipate that happening?

COUNSEL FOR THE GOVERNMENT: No, I do not, your Honor. The agency was directed to begin accepting requests for deferred action I believe beginning sometime in -- by mid-February but even after that we wouldn't anticipate any decisions on those for some time thereafter. So there -- I really would not expect anything between now and the date of the hearing.

Case 1:14-cv-00254 Document 347 Filed in TXSD on 05/19/16 Page 7 of 28

8

[Doc. No. 184 at 10–11] (emphasis added). Clearly, counsel for the Plaintiff States was concerned about

any intervening implementation of the 2014 DHS Directive that might occur before the injunction

hearing. The Government has now conceded that, at the very time counsel told the Court and opposing

counsel that no action was taking place, over 100,000 three-year deferred action renewals were being

processed using the 2014 DHS Directive.

The response by a DOJ lawyer, who the Government concedes knew that the DHS was already

issuing three-year extensions pursuant to the 2014 DHS directive, was:

"I really would not expect anything between now and the date of the hearing."

[Doc. No. 184 at 11] (emphasis added). How the Government can categorize the granting of over

100,000 applications as not being "anything" is beyond comprehension. Even if one did not think the

increase in DACA time limits was at issue, a position completely unjustifiable under the circumstances,

the duty of candor to the Court would certainly require that one mention the fact that the DHS was going

forward with that part of the 2014 DHS Directive.

This was not a curve ball thrown by the Government; this was a spitball which neither the

Plaintiff States nor the Court would learn of until March 3, 2015.

2. The January 2015 Misrepresentations

 One misrepresentation could be understandably a mistake, but the exchange between Counsel

and the Court in the January hearing puts to rest any doubt regarding misconduct. On this occasion, the

Court was worried about what impact a delay in the briefing schedule requested by the Government

might cause.

THE COURT: I'm a little concerned about how much time you asked for. If I give you until the 28th [of January, 2015], can you work with that?

COUNSEL FOR THE GOVERNMENT: Let me confer with my co-counsel, but I believe so.

9

Your Honor, in part we're just discussing about the need to respond to some of the voluminous factual material. If we could have until the 30th, that Friday, that would be preferable.

THE COURT: Okay. And . . . I guess to preempt Mr. Oldham [Counsel for the Plaintiff States] when I ask him does he have any problem with that, he's going to want to know what's happening when?

COUNSEL FOR THE GOVERNMENT: And we set this -- we did file yesterday afternoon, Your Honor.

THE COURT: I can't find it.

COUNSEL FOR THE GOVERNMENT: My apologies.

THE COURT: No, no. It's here. I just buried it with all my paper.

COUNSEL FOR THE GOVERNMENT: In that document [Motion for Extension of Time, Doc. No. 90] we reiterated that no applications for the revised DACA -- this is not even DAPA -- revised DACA would be accepted until the 18th of February, and that no action would be taken on any of those applications until March the 4th.

THE COURT: And nothing is happening on DAPA?

COUNSEL FOR THE GOVERNMENT: So the memorandum said that DAPA should be implemented no sooner than mid[-]May, so DACA is really the first -- the revised DACA is the first deadline.

THE COURT: Okay. Then you can have until the 30th.

COUNSEL FOR THE GOVERNMENT: Okay. Thank you.

THE COURT: Wait, wait. You're being flagged.

COUNSEL FOR THE GOVERNMENT: Oh, sorry. Just to be clear, I meant no later than. So the memorandum provides that by mid[-]May, DAPA will be stood up.

THE COURT: Okay.

COUNSEL FOR THE GOVERNMENT: But the main -- the driver here would be --

THE COURT: But as far as you know, nothing is going to happen in the next three weeks?

COUNSEL FOR THE GOVERNMENT: No, Your Honor.

Case 1:14-cv-00254 Document 347 Filed in TXSD on 05/19/16 Page 9 of 28

10

THE COURT: Okay. On either.

COUNSEL FOR THE GOVERNMENT: In terms of accepting applications or granting any up or down applications.

THE COURT: Okay.

COUNSEL FOR THE GOVERNMENT: For revised DACA, just to be totally clear.

[Doc. No. 106 at 133–34] (emphasis added).

Twice counsel for the Government (who, according to the Government's brief, knew that

the DHS was already granting renewals using revised DACA) told this Court that the

Government would not begin to implement the revised DACA (which includes the three-year

extensions) until mid-February. She, in fact, confirmed to this Court that nothing was going to

happen.

Certainly no one can claim this even approaches candor to the Court. This was not a

casual exchange between counsel. This exchange was prompted by the Government's own

request for additional time. It was responsive to a direct inquiry by the Court, which was

concerned that its order would, regardless of which side it ultimately favored, be issued in a

timely and fair fashion.

The reason this Court is certain that there could have been no misinterpretation as to whether the increase to a three-year renewal period was at issue is that it raised that very topic

just before the above-quoted exchange.

I know "legal speak" is boring and difficult sometimes to follow. I feel this was necessary though to prove to what lengths Obama and Hillary will go to achieve their goals. Here the Judge shows the Department of Justice Attorneys lying to protect Obama's Executive Order on Immigration, and even brings up where they did the same type things in the IRS Targeting scandal!

No matter what side you are on in the Immigration debate, you must realize violating the Constitution and lying to a Federal Judge is not an appropriate way to force the type immigration reform you desire. Is this really what you want your children and grandchildren to learn from your elected or appointed officials?

It is not only the right or wrong of lying to get your way. It is also the danger. When an administration lies and violates the Constitution, they take a very real chance on pushing this country into a Constitutional Crisis. At this point voters on both sides of the aisle are so angry I feel we are on the verge of that happening.

It is also the danger of not securing our borders and of releasing convicted criminals who happen to also be illegal aliens instead of deporting them immediately.

Not only did the Obama Administration by-pass Congress in direct violation of the Constitution, they also freed tens of thousands of illegal immigrants convicted of violent and serious crimes in 2013, according to the government's own records.

The crimes committed by illegal aliens released from federal custody include homicide, sexual assault, theft, kidnapping and alcohol-related driving convictions. In all, Immigration and Customs Enforcement (ICE) freed 36,007 aliens convicted of 88,000 crimes from detention centers throughout the United States, according to their own records!

The Washington D.C.-based group, Center for Immigration Studies (CIS), published a chart with a breakdown of the crimes committed by the illegal aliens who now roam freely in U.S. neighborhoods. The majority of the releases from ICE custody were discretionary, CIS found, which means they weren't required by law. In some instances the releases were actually contrary to law and local illegal immigrant sanctuary policies did not play a role in the vast majority. This means that it's part of the Obama administration's broader amnesty policy, which has favored letting illegal aliens live outside detention centers while their cases get resolved.

The records show that more than 16,000 were convicted of driving under the influence of drugs or alcohol. Over 9,000 had dangerous drug convictions, 1,075 were convicted of aggravated assault, 426 of sexual assault and 193 of homicide. Additionally, the records show that 1,160 of the freed illegal immigrants had stolen vehicle convictions, 303 kidnapping convictions and 303 flight escape convictions.

Thousands of others were convicted of lesser crimes that are nevertheless serious enough to merit detention if you're already in the country illegally. Those offenses include extortion, embezzlement, arson, domestic violence, property crimes, larceny, burglary, intimidation, obstructing police, weapon offenses, forgery, obstructing the judiciary and a variety of fraud. Those who take the time to read the entire list may find it difficult to imagine that the government would even consider freeing these offenders.

Incredibly, it's not the first time this happens. The feds previously released 68,000 different criminal aliens encountered by ICE officers in jails that were let go instead of processed for deportation, according to records obtained by CIS. This latest batch of 36,007 is a group of aliens who were being processed for removal and were freed while awaiting the final disposition of their cases. Despite their serious criminal convictions, they were released by means of bond, order of recognizance, order of supervision, parole or alternative detention such as an ankle bracelet.

"The document raises questions about the Obama administration's management of enforcement resources, as well as its enforcement plans and priorities," CIS logically concludes. As examples, the group offers a recent ICE directive (prosecutorial discretion) and policy (Deferred Action for Childhood Arrivals) which make broad categories of illegal immigrants immune to enforcement. "These policies have forced ICE officers in the field to avoid or cease deportation action in thousands of cases, even in cases of aliens charged with or convicted of crimes," CIS reveals.

This is hardly the first time that the government rewards illegal immigrants with serious criminal records. Last summer Judicial Watch reported that legislation crafted by the bipartisan Gang of Eight in the U.S. Senate would grant amnesty to illegal aliens with drunk-driving, domestic violence, aggravated assault and child abuse convictions.

Hillary has claimed in campaign speech after campaign speech she intends to follow in Obama's footsteps in regards to Immigration. Is that really what you want in another President? Someone who doesn't care about violating the Constitution? Someone who's DOJ Lawyers are forced to go to ethics classes because they lied to the Court? They should have been disbarred and criminally prosecuted. Does anyone reading this think for one minute if you had lied to a Federal Judge in open court you wouldn't have been prosecuted?

It is not only that, but some of those released have gone on to commit murder and other crimes.

A few examples:

Apolinar Altamirano, 29, an unauthorized Mexican illegal alien DREAMer, has been arrested for the January 22, 2015 first-degree murder of Phoenix Quick Trip store clerk Grant Ronnebeck, 21.

Altamirano is accused of shooting Ronnebeck and stealing two packs of cigarettes after the 21-year-old clerk demanded payment before giving Altamirano any cigarettes.

The murder was recorded on the store's security camera and police captured Altamirano after a high speed chase in Phoenix. Altamirano had previous run-ins with local police and Immigration and Customs Enforcement. In 2012, he pleaded guilty to facilitation to commit burglary and got probation but was placed in deportation proceedings.

 Before the murder of Ronnebeck, Altamirano was released on a $10,000 bond in 2013 from ICE custody despite the defendant's own claims of ties to the Mexican Mafia. After his release, but before Ronnebeck's murder, Altamirano also allegedly threatened to kill two people, resulting in harassment injunctions against Altamirano.

Altamirano reportedly entered the U.S. illegally at the age of 14 and prior to his arrest, worked illegally as a landscaper.

Emily Cortez 7-week-old baby, was killed by Laura Flores-Santillan, 49, a Mexican national illegally living in Akron Ohio, has pled guilty (via an interpreter) to child endangering and reckless homicide. In a special pleading called an Alford plea, Santillan avoids a possible life sentence for murder.

Santillan now faces a maximum of 11 years in prison and deportation to Mexico after she serves her prison sentence. Santillan reportedly has lived in the US illegally for 11 years and was an in-home daycare operator. Baby Cortez was in the care of Santillan after which the baby ended up on a ventilator at the Akron Children's Hospital. Baby Cortez died several days later. Prosecutors were prepared to have medical experts testify that Baby Cortez suffered severe head injuries from blunt force trauma while in the care of Santillan.

Juan Jimenez-Olivera, 30, a Mexican national illegally living in Hillsborough, New Jersey, has pled guilty to theft, aggravated arson, corpse desecration, and the strangulation murder of Sviartlana Dranko, 30.

Olivera knew the victim because they both worked at the same pizzeria. Olivera strangled Dranko to death after an apparent sexual assault at her home in Hillsborough in April, 2014. Olivera is believed to have tried to cover up the theft of $6,000 and the murder by setting Dranko's body on fire.

Eventually Olivera admitted to the murder, theft, and lying to police about the murder. Olivera's previous $1 million bail has been revoked and awaits sentencing. Members of victim's family attended Olivera's guilty plea court hearing.

Then there is this from the Texas DPS webpage on crimes by foreign nationals:

"From October 2008 through July 1, 2014, Texas has identified a total of 203,685 unique criminal alien defendants booked into Texas county jails. Over their criminal careers, these defendants are responsible for at least 642,564 individual criminal charges mostly consisting of Class B misdemeanors or higher, including 3,070 homicides and 7,964 sexual assaults,"

The same as with Obama's early release program from Federal Prisons. Something else Hillary has promised to continue.

A death penalty indictment has been filed against a convicted cocaine dealer after police say he murdered his ex-girlfriend and her two children after having been granted an early prison release.

These are the kind of things that can happen when your release convicts early.

On March 3, 2016 a grand jury indicted Wendell Callahan, 35, is charged with the triple-murder of Erveena Hammonds, 32, and her two young daughters, Anaesia Green, 10, and Breya Hammonds, 7. Police said that Callahan brutally stabbed the three victims to death inside of their home in north Columbus, Ohio, in January.

Callahan would have been still serving a nearly 13-year federal prison sentence at the time of the murders if he had not been released early due to a change in sentencing guidelines. As Judicial Watch noted, the change occurred as part of President Barack Obama's criminal justice reform efforts and an attempt to end racial discrimination.

Chapter 10 - The Damage Done by Obama and Clinton Standard

Perhaps the most lasting damage done to America by Barack Obama and Hillary Clinton is their attitude of it doesn't matter what lies they have to tell, or laws they must break as long as they get their way. This will have long lasting negative consequences on our country. In this final chapter we are going to look at the many instances of this behavior and the *proof* this happened over and over.

A statement by President Barack Obama was given the dubious honor of "Lie of the Year" with a rating of "Pants on Fire" by the Tampa Bay Times' Politifact.

"If you like your health care plan, you can keep it," the president said, over and over again, while trying to sell Americans on the Affordable Care Act before it was passed. It was a promise to American citizens that the law would not affect their current insurance policies.

Who can forget "If you like your Dr. you can keep your Dr."

"But the promise was impossible to keep," Politifact said in its announcement.

Cancellation letters sent to four million Americans notifying them that under Obamacare they could not in fact, keep their health insurance prompted the president to issue an extremely rare apology. He claimed no one could have known of these reactions. Guess what? Later we found out even that statement was a lie.

In November 2014, a series of videos emerged of Gruber speaking about the ACA at different events, from 2010 to 2013, in ways that showed how the American public was lied to and mis-led. Many of the videos show him talking about ways in which he felt the ACA was misleadingly crafted or marketed in order to get the bill passed, while in some of the videos he specifically refers to American voters as ill-informed or "stupid". In the first, most widely-publicized video taken at a panel discussion about the ACA at the University of Pennsylvania in October 2013, Gruber said the bill was deliberately written "in a tortured way" to disguise the fact that it creates a system by which "healthy people pay in and sick people get money". He said this was needed due to "the stupidity of the American voter" in order to sell it to the public. Gruber said the bill's designed "lack of transparency is a huge political advantage" in selling it. The comments caused a huge outcry! In two other videos, Gruber was shown talking about the decision to have the bill tax insurance companies instead of patients (the so-called "Cadillac tax"), which he called fundamentally the same thing economically but more palatable politically. In one video, he stated that "the American people are too stupid to understand the difference" between the two approaches, while in the other he said that the switch worked due to "the lack of economic understanding of the American voter". He also said John Kerry was the one who came up with this idea. One has to wonder how much money this would save the Heinz Corporation. In another video, taken in 2010, Gruber expressed doubts that the ACA would significantly reduce health care costs, though he noted that lowering costs played a major part in the way the bill was promoted. In another video, taken in 2011, Gruber again talks about manipulation behind the "Cadillac tax", this time also stating that the tax is designed so that, though it begins by affecting only 8% of insurance plans, it will "over the next 20 years" come to apply to nearly all employer-provided health plans.

Before the Gruber video came out Obama and his surrogates were busy claiming it was an honest mistake. The videos show no, it was all just a lie so he could get his way, no matter the cost. At first they tried to discredit Gruber. Fortunately for us when you are paid by the government there is a paper trail. Gruber was under a $297,000 contract with the U.S. Department of Health and Human Services. Not to mention contracts with various State Governments.

Obviously trying to say he had very little to do with it wasn't going to work. Especially after a video came up with Obama citing Gruber's work. Then from his surrogates came the so what if he lied he at least got healthcare passed and look at all the people who now have healthcare.

The second promise made in selling Obamacare was that the reform would lower health insurance premiums. Politifact rated the President's statement that the ACA would reduce the cost of health care "half true." For some Americans, premiums will go down, and for others the premiums will go up. The Affordable Care Act's changes are raising insurance premiums for some people who did well under the old system and lowering them for some of the people who were locked out or discriminated against." Who are these losers? The 15 million Americans who are on the individual market, many of whom are small business owners, and will now have to pay more. The young and healthy who wanted minimal coverage before, will be forced to pay higher premiums to subsidize the cost of the expanded insurance pool with older and sicker patients.

On to the lie of saying the ACA would save the average family $2,500.00 per year. When selling the law, the President never made such important caveats. As Megan McCardle points out, in 2008 the President said that his plan would save $2,500 annually for families through a "combination of developing efficiencies in the system, expanding coverage to all Americans, and picking up the cost of some high-cost cases." On December 15, 2009, the president said, "Families will save on their premiums," and added that if the law is not passed, "premiums are guaranteed to go up." There was no mention of lowering the rates of some on the backs of the young and small-business owners on the self-insurance market. Even in 2009, policy analysts recognized that there would be winners and losers of the law. But there was a total lack of communication on who would be worse off. No time for facts when selling this law, only lies and half-truths.

The third main promise, repeated many times, was that the Affordable Care Act would not impose a tax increase. Remember, in 2009, the president un-categorically denied to George Stephanopoulos that the Affordable Care Act imposed a tax increase? Had the law been called a tax, the president could never have mustered the votes to pass it. Senate Minority Leader Mitch McConnell said the the tax-free ACA "was one of the Democrats' top selling points. Why you ask? Because they knew it would have never passed if they said it was a tax increase.

It didn't take long for the administration to break this promise, much like so many of their promises. Within months of passing the law, in court the Department of Justice took the opposite position, and insisted that the law was constitutional because it was a tax increase. And it was on that basis that Chief Justice Roberts upheld the law. Even to this day, the Obama administration maintains in court that Obamacare is a tax, but denies it to the American voter.

At the time the Affordable Care Act was being debated, 86% of those who had insurance were happy with their insurance plan. A more disturbing fact, in spite of their lies to the contrary, the Administration *knew* as many as 93 million Americans will over time lose their plans. The truth doesn't matter to them, the only thing that matters is getting their way.

Hillary's finger prints are all over this too. She has bragged on the ACA on the campaign trail in the past year. She has said she intends to take it even further. In spite of the President and Democratic promises to the contrary even said she plans to make it available to illegal immigrants. Hillary has her own "Lie of the Year." Several of them actually.

Benghazi. I'm not going to deep into this. I have read the book "13 Hours" seen the movie and read the 800 page House Benghazi report. You all can do the same and make your own opinions. I just want to touch on the lie she told two parents on the tarmac at Dover Air Force base in front of their son's flag draped coffins.

Patricia Smith, the mother of State Department information specialist Sean Smith, has publically stated numerous times Hillary lied to her. She claims Hillary told her the attack was because of the video, and they were going to prosecute the man who made the video. Hillary denies she said that to Mrs. Smith, however in 2013, in testimony to the House Government Affairs Committee, Smith said every prominent administration official at the event blamed the attack on a video:

"Obama and Hillary and Panetta and Biden and Susan all came up to me at the casket ceremony. Every one of them came up to me, gave me a big hug and I asked them what happened, please tell me. And every one of them said, it was the video. And we all know that it wasn't the video, even at that time they knew it wasn't the video. So they all lied to me."

In an interview with Lars Lawson, Ty Woods Father said, "Well, this is what Hillary did. She came over and, you know, she did the same thing. You know, separately came over and talked with me. I gave her a hug, shook her hand. And she did not appear to be one bit sincere at all, and, you know, she mentioned that thing about, 'We're going to have that person arrested and prosecuted that did the video.' That was the first time I had even heard anything like that."

In an interview on "The Blaze," Woods quoted Clinton as saying: "We will make sure that the person who made that film is arrested and prosecuted."

Mr. Woods even produced his day calendar where he documented his conversation the day it happened.

Yet another strange comment from Hillary in the hanger that day. Kate Quigley, the sister of Glen Doherty, said that in her conversation with Clinton, the then-secretary of state made no mention of a video, but did refer to a "spontaneous protest."

"She said we had to be sorry for the Libyan people because they are uneducated, and that breeds fear, which breeds violence, and leads to spontaneous protests and acts of violence," Quigley said in an interview. "The point was that it was not a planned thing; it just happened."

Quigley said that "it seemed strange to tell us to have sympathy for the Libyan people."

Doesn't sound like the thing to say to a woman at a time when her brother's flag draped coffin is present.

Libya. It was supposed to be Hillary's crowning achievement. It should be her Waterloo. Not only because of Benghazi. The "Lead from Behind" strategy developed by Hillary and Obama has led to another failed state. Another safe haven for Islamic terrorists. The last knowledgeable estimate I heard is 5,000 ISIS fighters in Libya alone. This doesn't count Al-Qaeda and other Islamic terrorists.

We will hopefully never forget the video of the Coptic Christians being marched out to the beach forced to kneel, then be-headed. I will never forget the 13 hours of Benghazi. The other horror stories from Libya.

On October 19, 2015 a Christian was be-headed on video by ISIS. April 19, 2015 The Islamic State releases a video showing the brutal execution of thirty captured Ethiopian Christians, at least a dozen of whom are beheaded. December 23, 2014, ISIS murders a Christian couple and abduct their daughter. So typical of Islamic terrorists.

I could go on and on with this list, but I hope you get the point. When the USA leads from behind and creates a vacuum, the result is never good. Just as when Obama pulled out and abandoned Iraq.

We have all heard Hillary say she turned over all of her work related emails. She never sent or received any classified emails on her server. Then she changed it to any that were marked classified at the time. That she only used one device.

Look at this transcript from the FBI Director's sworn testimony before Congress answering questions from Congressman Trey Gowdy:

Gowdy: "Secretary Clinton said there was nothing marked classified on her emails, either sent or received. Is that true?"

Comey: "That's not true, there were a small number of portion markings on, I think, three of the documents."

Gowdy:"Secretary Clinton said, 'I did not email any classified material to anyone on my email, there is no classified material.' Was that true?"

Comey: "There was classified material emailed."

Gowdy: "Secretary Clinton said she used just one device. Was that true?"

Comey: "She used multiple devices during the four years of her term as secretary of state."

Gowdy: "Secretary Clinton said all work-related emails were returned to the State Department. Was that true?"

Comey: "No, we found work-related emails, thousands that were not returned."

Sounds like she lied to Congress to me, which is perjury.

18 U.S. Code § 1621 - Perjury generally

Whoever—

(1) having taken an oath before a competent tribunal, officer, or person, in any case in which a law of the United States authorizes an oath to be administered, that he will testify, declare, depose, or certify truly, or that any written testimony, declaration, deposition, or certificate by him subscribed, is true, willfully and contrary to such oath states or subscribes any material matter which he does not believe to be true; or

(2) in any declaration, certificate, verification, or statement under penalty of perjury as permitted under section 1746 of title 28, United States Code, willfully subscribes as true any material matter which he does not believe to be true;

is guilty of perjury and shall, except as otherwise expressly provided by law, be fined under this title or imprisoned not more than five years, or both. This section is applicable whether the statement or subscription is made within or without the United States.

The concept that it is permissible to lie in order to achieve your goals has gone through this entire

Administration like a bad virus. Had common Americans been caught in these lies they would now reside in prison.

Another prime example of Obama being willing to tell any lie to get his way. David Axelrod writes in his book, "Believer," the president had "compromised his position" on same-sex marriage in 2008 when he said he favored civil unions over full marriage equality for same-sex couples.

In response to the book, Obama said in an interview with BuzzFeed News he had "always felt" that same-sex couples should be afforded equal rights and that it was "frustrating to me not to, I think, be able to square that with what were a bunch of religious sensitivities there."

Basically Obama said Axelrod's claims weren't true, but then in the interview claimed because of "religious sensitivities" he was frustrated he couldn't admit publically he supported same sex marriage during the campaign. In plain English, he had to lie to the American people to achieve his agenda. Then he lied to the American people again when he said his position had evolved. That his daughters had caused him to re-think his position. No matter your position on same sex marriage, it is wrong for any politician to intentionally lie to the American people to achieve their agenda.

As documented in the chapter "Iran" numerous lies were told for Obama and Hillary to achieve their goals on the treaty with Iran. Yes the so called negotiations began while Hillary was still Secretary of State. Yes Kerry carried on the tradition of lying to the American people to achieve the treaty. Yes they used the press to try to fool the American people. It is well documented in the New York Times. It isn't documented because of good reporting. It is documented once again because of an Obama advisor bragging about it!

In my opinion, these are the horrible damages done to our country. We have a crop of politicians, led by Obama and the Clintons that have decided no lie is too big, provided it pushes their agenda. The only thing that matters is increasing their net worth and getting away with violating the Constitution, violating the letter of the law, and pushing their liberal, socialist agenda.

Guantanamo Bay is one more in series of such lies. Just more lies. More propaganda all to help Obama keep a campaign promise. There is already over 30% of the prisoners released who have returned to terror. Now he is releasing the worst of the worst. Does anyone believe that percentage won't increase? There is already sworn testimony Americans have been killed by the hands of some of those who have been released. Now that we are down to the very worst does anyone honestly believe their release won't cause even more dangers to Americans? More loss of life?

What I don't understand is how even loyal Democrats can be for Obama, Hillary and Kerry's lies that have and will cost more American lives. Is keeping an ill-advised campaign promise really worth the loss of life?

Please, before you vote in the next election, remember what you have read in this book. Do your own research.

Read the Constitution. I am not saying Donald Trump was my first choice. He wasn't. Not even close. Out of the 17 Republican candidates when the primary first started I only rated 2 below him. A vote for anyone but him, or a non-vote however, in spite of what never Trump people say is as bad as a vote for Hillary. In my opinion Hillary is much worse than Obama.

After reading Obama's books I think he lies and does what he does because he is a "True Believer." He really thinks America has done wrong throughout history and that he is the anointed one pre-destined to right the wrongs done by America. As such he thinks it is ok for him to lie and deceive the American public. He is after all on a mission. He thinks it is his place in History to make America pay for her past sins, and as Michelle Obama said, make him proud of America for the first time.

I totally disagree with him in so many ways. That being said at least he believes what he does. Not so with Hillary. She is in it simply for power and greed. It is not me saying it. She has been saying it through her actions in her career. Her entire adult life has been one filled with nothing but acquiring more power and more wealth. She has lied to the American people since her days as a young attorney. She will continue to do that if you, the American voter, allow this evil woman to become President of the United States of America.

No matter what you think of Donald Trump, there is no way he can be as bad for America as Hillary Clinton can.

ABOUT THE AUTHOR

This is Danny's 5th book. He also has written a small group study guide for his first 2 books. Danny is not a trained author. He is simply a Christian and an America loving citizen.

Before Danny's accident in 1997, he had been in Law Enforcement. He worked as a Patrol Officer, an Investigator and a Police Chief. When he left Law Enforcement he had a successful career in business. He was a sales rep, a regional sales manager, a national sales and operations manager.

In 1997, after a fall from the roof of his house, he began an intense study of The Bible and in 2005 started Preaching and speaking at Churches. He also began an in-depth study of Islam in 2003.

His study of Islam has led him to acquire over 140 books on the subject and inspired him to share the Gospel of Jesus Christ to everyone he comes into contact with, especially working hard to introduce the Jesus Christ of the Holy Bible to the followers of Islam.

Other books by Danny:
America's Holy War, One Christian's View of Islam
Modern Day Christian Martyrs
We Owe it to Our Children, Time to Take Back Our Country.
Looking Back at Myself, My Life and Testimony

Danny can be reached at WeOweItToOurChildren@aol.com